SEVEN STARS

THE OLDEST
LICENSED HOUSE
IN GREAT BRITAIN
LICENSED OVER 540 YEARS

SEVEN STARS

ANCIENT ASTRONOMY
AND THE
ENGLISH PUBLIC HOUSE

HUGH KOLB

UNICORN

Published in 2019 by Unicorn
an imprint of Unicorn Publishing Group LLP
5 Newburgh Street, London W1F 7RG

www.unicornpublishing.org

ISBN 978-1-911604-97-6

10 9 8 7 6 5 4 3 2 1

Designed by Dr Hugh Kolb
Printed in China

CONTENTS

INTRODUCTION 7

THE ORIGINS OF THE PUB 9

INN SIGNS 21

SEVEN STARS 35

THE IMMACULATE CONCEPTION 127

THE BOOK OF ENOCH 141

THE MASONS 151

THE SOLAR SYSTEM 157

THE PLOUGH 167

THE SEVEN STARS OF TAURUS 173

STARS AND MONASTERIES 187

THE ANGLO-SAXONS AND THE DANES 203

THE CELESTIAL GRAPES 211

CONCLUSIONS 223

APPENDICES 229
NOTES 233
BIBLIOGRAPHY 235
INDEX 238

INTRODUCTION

Many histories of inns and taverns have been written over the past 150 years. These have inevitably concentrated on the most scenic and architecturally interesting or those that have prominent backstories, the more lurid the better. Famous old coaching inns with complex half-timbered fronts and sporting elaborate wooden carvings or plaster panels have interested writers since the days of Charles Harper, who published numerous surveys of English inns as rendezvous for the new-fangled breed of cyclists at the end of the nineteenth century. With the advent of the modern car (and before drink-driving laws became the hallmark of the caring state), numerous gazetteers of rural road houses and scenic country pubs showed the more affluent where to spend their weekends and holidays. Any hostelry that had attracted historical (and usually well-heeled) figures from Good Queen Bess and Bonny Prince Charlie to Jack Hawkins and Lord Nelson, or had been mentioned by William Shakespeare or Samuel Pepys, demanded attention. The majority of small inns and local bars without any marked architectural features, homicidal landlords or regular ghosts have not been worth consideration, however old they might claim to be.

Nobody has thought it worthwhile to publish histories of particular names or signs — a survey of Saracen's Heads or a study of Horse and Ploughs — for their own sake. Admittedly, there is a limited mileage to be got out of such establishments as the King's and Queen's Heads. The number of candidates is limited and well known. Apart from a discussion of the politics and psychology of patriotism or whether the Elephant and Castle really was the Infanta of Castile, there is little to add.

Antiquarians and social historians have produced a number of studies of inn signs in general, starting with Larwood and Hotten's *The History of Signboards from the Earliest Times to the Present Day* first published in 1866. These have generally been more interested in the exotic and decorative rather than the everyday and are weak on provenance and meaning. Bryant Lillywhite's *London Signs* is comprehensive in its area and provides short explanations of the possible meanings of signs but many of these are inevitably speculative or superficial. When it comes to the Seven Stars they are definitely wrong, repeating errors that have been circulating in the printed media for several hundred years and which are now being perpetuated in the internet age.

The Seven Stars stand out as a special case. Compared to many other images used for pub signs, the depiction of seven stars has a wide range of cultural and literary associations. This is the main reason why so many conflicting explanations have been provided for the meaning of the name. Seven stars appear in religious and astronomical

*Frontpiece:
Ye Olde
Seven Stars,
Withy Grove
Manchester in
1908*

*Opposite:
The Seven Stars,
Robertsbridge*

contexts that can be traced back to the first millennium BC and before. They appear in the Bible and other fringe religious texts from our Judaeo-Christian inheritance. They have been adopted by the Freemasons, a fraternity with an insatiable predilection for symbols of all kinds. They appear in many other political and religious settings, which makes it difficult to pin down one single explanation for their use as an inn sign. It is only by a concentrated analysis of the surviving pubs, their history and the symbolism of the Seven Stars over the past three thousand years that we can arrive at any sort of conclusion. The present book attempts to do this.

The Seven Stars, Foots Cray in the 1950's

THE ORIGINS OF THE PUB

Any liquid that contains sugar can be used to grow yeast. This widespread and useful fungal micro-organism has two main forms of excreta: carbon dioxide and ethyl alcohol. The first allows us to make one of the staffs of life, leavened bread, the other beer and wine. The two natural sources of sugar are fruits and honey. A more plentiful supply can be obtained by germinating and then cooking cereal grains to release sugar from complex carbohydrates. The result is fermented by the yeast to produce a relaxing or intoxicating drink. Such alcoholic beverages, whether they be ale and beer brewed mainly from barley, wine from fermented grapes, or similar drinks obtained from a wide variety of grains, fruits and saps, are part of the human condition and have been appreciated by most cultures throughout history even when other vegetable intoxicants were available. A number of higher animals have been shown to select fermented fruit in preference to a fresh supply because of its alcohol content. Presumably early humans did the same long before the ideas of organised viniculture and agriculture arrived. For many years it was thought that living in permanent townships originally began because people found they could grow a surplus of cereals. This increased their food supply throughout the year and left time free for a settled existence where they could pursue cultural activities beyond mere hunting and gathering, such as making pots for brewing beer and fermenting more wine. Such ideas are changing.

The oldest known human monument is Göbekli Tepe in south-eastern Turkey. It is a collection of carved T-shaped pillars in circular enclosures dating from the Pre-pottery Neolithic, around BC 9000. There is no evidence of any living quarters associated with it. Villages did not appear in the area until the eighth century, and the first large town, Çatal Höyük, was built around BC 6000. Within the remains of Göbekli Tepe there are several large stone vats which could each contain up to 160 litres of liquid. Based on some tentative chemical analyses it is claimed that these show the residues of ritual brewing. The infill of the site also contains numerous animal bones. The argument put forward from this research is that seasonal feasting and drinking at specific religious sites was the trigger for bringing people together from their previously more isolated hunter-gatherer existence and was the source of later Neolithic organisation and, eventually, civilisation.[1] The original purpose of selecting and deliberately growing cereals was not to make bread but to brew ale, although we might not recognise the result. It was probably an alcoholic barley gruel or porridge but, for all that, as or more nutritious than much else that was available with the added benefits of producing a good time and allowing people the apparent experience of communing with higher forces in the cosmos.

Communal drinking has carried on throughout history, from the symposia of the Greeks, the autumnal binges of the Persians and the feast days of the Vikings, down to the weddings, Christmases and Hogmanays of the modern world. In parallel with these, however, there have been establishments where people could go to spend a sociable evening drinking and, if necessary, eat or stay the night. They existed in ancient Egypt and Mesopotamia. We know about them mainly because of comments by elite writers that they might be a source of drunkenness, social ills, prostitution and subversive political meetings, and from the laws that were set down to control them.

Barley beer became a staple for life in Egypt and the Middle East. It was part of the daily allowance for all public servants, workers and soldiers, and was almost certainly healthier than drinking water straight from rivers and canals. More sophisticated wines were the reserve of the elite. One of the earliest civilisations that we know about is that of Sumeria, now southern Iraq. The first record of beer is on Sumerian temple accounts from the fourth millennium BC. These are a mixture of pictographic and numerical signs impressed into clay tablets. Signs that have been interpreted as representing barley groats, malt and jars appear on the same tablets in quantities of over 100,000 litres with the characters of an official who certified the record.[2] Different jar signs suggest that several varieties of beer were being produced and one tablet notes the ingredients for eight different brews. The Sumerians even had a Goddess of Beer: Ninkasi. A poem lauding her survives from around BC 1800 which is essentially a recipe for brewing in eight stages. Mind you, too much should not be made of this because the Sumerians were determined polytheists and had deities for everything from the major celestial bodies and earthly forces down to bricks and saw blades.

The first images of beer drinking are on cylinder seals from the Early Dynastic period of Sumeria during the third millennium BC. These show figures sucking up drink from large pots through a straw.[3] Other images picture people or gods drinking what was probably wine from cups and bowls. One such lapis lazuli seal found by Sir Leonard Woolley in the Royal Cemetery at Ur shows people drinking beer and wine, and another two transporting

The images on a cylinder seal from Ur dating to the third millennium BC showing people drinking beer and wine, and transporting a large jug

a large pot suspended from a pole on what appears to be a quite sophisticated two-wheeled cart. This suggests that brewing was carried out somewhere else and the beer was distributed to alehouses rather than being made on the premises. The complex recipes involving mixing dough with dates, baking it, soaking it with malted grain in large vats to make wort, brewing it and then draining through reed mats would indicate that centralised production was the most practical method.

The Babylonian Law Code of King Hammurabi, engraved on a stone pillar around BC 1775, set down four regulations out of a total of 282 for these alehouse keepers: *sabitum* in Old Babylonian — written in the characters of the older Sumerian language as **munus lu kaš din na**, literally 'female beer-selling person'. Patrons could get credit for beer and repay with an equivalent amount of barley. The volume of grain for a corresponding quantity of drink was specified. If the landlady accepted silver money instead and overcharged, she could be thrown into the Euphrates, probably attached to a few weights to make things more interesting. This was a religiously based ordeal in which final judgment was left to the 'holy river'. If she drowned the river god had agreed with the verdict. A priestess who set up an alehouse or was found drinking in one was to be burnt to death. Any landlady who overheard political conspirators in her establishment and did not report it to the royal court could be summarily executed. For a variety of reasons, in our more enlightened times, publicans no longer face the prospect of capital punishment in their line of business.

The gender of the language used in Hammurabi's Laws show that it was mainly women in Babylon who sold and possibly made the beer. This is reinforced by the original beer deity being a goddess, which makes it strange that priestesses should have been subject to such stringent regulation. Perhaps it was due more to do whom they might associate rather than with any drinking they did. Later Assyrian references to brewing and selling beer often use the masculine form, *sabu*, so men must have been involved as well.

A typical Middle Eastern alehouse seems to have consisted of people sitting around a large pot and sucking up beer through straws, a practice still found in parts of east Africa. This basic filtration system prevents you getting mouthfuls of the barley husks and suchlike crud which are still floating about in the brew. Apart from this, we know very little about such premises. Developing urban societies drew people in from the countryside. Many would have lived in one room hovels so they required external services for eating and drinking. They also socialised more frequently than people in rural areas. The new cities temporarily accommodated traders and carters from round about to provide supplies and were centres of administration which needed to communicate with other cities and exchange personnel. It is only in Roman times that we start to get a clearer picture of this sector of the leisure and travel industry and how it operated.

We are told in the Gospel of St Luke that there were inns in the town of Bethlehem in the time of Caesar Augustus. In the rest of the empire the Romans had *deversoria* and *hospes* on the main roads which offered higher class accommodation for officials and bona fide travellers. *Cauponae* provided basic food, drink and accommodation, often near city gates. *Tabernae* sold wine but could also have more general goods, and *popinae* were cook shops for eating in. There were also *ganeae,* which were more disreputable eating houses. All these categories overlapped. The *popina* served liquid refreshment and looked more like a bar. The *taberna* may have been a *taberna vinaria* that sold wine or a *taberna devertere* and *taberna meritoria* that offered lodgings. The *caupona* (and even the *popina*) was often a part-time brothel, although nominally distinct from the *fornix, lupanar* or *stabulum* where, according to Petronius' *Satyricon,* naked girls lined up with price tags round their necks. The *popinae* were particularly associated with gambling.

After being buried under the lava and ash from an eruption of Mount Vesuvius in AD 79 the city of Pompeii gives us a time capsule for this period of Mediterranean culture. Partial excavations have shown that there were thirty-four *cauponae*, 125 *popinae* and nine brothels in an area of 44 ha.[4] The population of the whole city was only around 10,000. Many of the *popinae* were very small with a single room facing the street, fronted by a bar counter containing recessed jars for food and wine (*dolia*) and a cooking area at one end. By contrast, some of the *cauponae* were extensive with a garden or yard for carts, and attached buildings for cooking and accommodation. Out in the countryside the same businesses stayed closer to their core functions and were less involved in licentious behaviour.

Fermented alcoholic drinks must have come into Britain with the first people after the last glaciation. Communal drinking was the norm until the Roman invasion when urbanised Mediterranean customs and better communications started to take over. Therefore the first alehouses, taverns and inns in England would have been based on the forms described above, albeit rather less exposed to the elements than their Mediterranean cousins.

Writing in his Natural History (around AD 60), Pliny the Elder considered wine to be the characteristic product of Italy and Greece. Drinks made from fermented grain were the preserve of Gaul and Spain, as well as Egypt. Greek settlers in southern France may have introduced some viticulture but it was the Roman emperor Probus who decreed that growing vines should be encouraged in Spain, Gaul and southern Germany (and, possibly, England) around AD 280. Nevertheless, there has always been a perceived distinction in Europe between northern beer drinkers and southern wine drinkers.

This is a simplification but does not alter the fact that most of the wine drunk in northern Europe, and particularly in England, had to be imported and was a more expensive merchandise which replaced mead (fermented honey) as the drink of the elite. By contrast, ale and beer have come to be seen as an expression of the grass root traditions of native northern cultures. This affected who drank what and where it was sold. Early historians of the wine trade, such as André Simon, suggested that serious wine drinking did not start in England until the Anglo-Saxon period when the Christian church established it as part of the sacrament. However, typical Roman wine *amphorae* are found in numbers in southern and south-east England from the second century BC onwards.[5]

ALE, BEER AND CIDER

The words 'ale' and 'beer' are often used interchangeably but for some people they are really quite distinct products. As we have seen, the fermenting of grain goes back to the beginnings of organised human culture but the brew had to be cooked up especially and drunk fairly quickly before it went off. In the Middle Ages other ingredients, particularly herbs but up to and including dead chickens, were included to increase the range of flavours. Some of the herbs that were used may have had additional psychoactive properties in addition to the basic alcohol. For instance, seeds of the henbane plant were sometimes included. It is said that such brews were favoured by witches who valued the effects of the powerful alkaloid hallucinogens involved.

Sometime during the ninth century monks in southern Germany and Switzerland discovered that by boiling the wort with hops and then using a few more to flavour it they could produce a more astringent brew that lasted much longer in storage because of the antiseptic effects of tannins in the mixture. Other chemicals in hop flowers induce mildly relaxing and soporific effects. Botanically, hop plants (*Humulus*) are closely related to *Cannabis*, but this never seems to have bothered anybody. For a long time herbalists have used such hops for promoting sleep and as an analgesic and sedative. Dried flowers were sometimes put into pillows. This new addition to the diet may have made the rigours of monastic and convent life more congenial.

In the English tradition the basic drink fermented without hops is generally referred to as ale whereas the addition of hops turns it into beer. The first record of hopped beer being imported into England was from Flanders in 1288. However, it did not find universal favour for several hundred years. Some people railed against the use of hops, regarding them as a pollutant of traditional ale. People could be fined for adulterating ale with hops up until the sixteenth century. Henry VIII forbade the royal brewer putting hops in his ale. As late as 1651, John Taylor, 'The Water Poet', could write:

> Beere is a Dutch Boorish Liquor, a thing not knowne in England, till of
> late dayes an Alien to our Nation.

People with a more European outlook nowadays tend to divide beers differently into ales and lagers, based on the fermentation process rather the ingredients. Ales are top fermented at room temperature whereas lagers are bottom fermented by a different species of yeast in near freezing conditions and then stored in the cold.[6] Ale and beer also had to compete with another popular drink: cider.

Cider seems to have been produced in England before the Romans arrived but it was the Normans who put it on a firm basis. While cider was made right across the south of England and the West Country, in the late Middle Ages Kent and Sussex were its two strongest areas. Cider production rivalled that of ale in the countryside and many farm workers received the drink daily as part of their wages. Nowadays we associate cider production with the West Country, particularly Somerset, but this is because the area was, until recently, relatively underdeveloped and kept hold of older customs. For instance, people like Cecil Sharp would travel round Somerset after 1900 to collect folk songs which had died out in the rest of England. It was the commercial brewing potential of hopped beer that eventually saw off cider and the apple orchards of Kent were replaced by fields of hops. At the last count there were only four committed cider houses left in England. The rise of hops in Kent can be roughly dated from Daniel Defoe's *A Tour Thro' the Whole Island of Great Britain* published in 1724:

> But the great wealth and encrease of the city of Canterbury, is from the surprising encrease of the hop grounds all around the place; it is within living memory of many of the inhabitants now living, and that none of the oldest neither, that there was not an acre ground planted with hops in the whole neighbourhood, or so few as not to be worth naming; whereas I was assured that there are at this time near six thousand acres of ground so planted, within a very few miles of the city.

The other main rivals to ale and beer in the eighteenth century were spirits. Gin and brandy (originating in Holland and France, respectively) had been available during the seventeenth century but it was the arrival of a Dutch monarch in William III that set in line a new trend. Taxes on beer were increased but restrictions on operating distilleries were removed. The result was an outbreak of hard drinking such as that satirised by William Hogarth in his 1751 engravings, *Gin Lane* and *Beer Street*. Much of the legislation concerning taxation and liquor licences over the next hundred years was concerned with trying to correct this imbalance and reduce the effects of gin shops. Outside England whisky was the spirit of choice in Ireland and Scotland. However, production of this was mainly a cottage industry until the big Victorian distillers came along.

ALEHOUSES AND TAVERNS

The standard triumvirate of the early drinks trade in England has always been alehouses, taverns and inns which respectively sold ale, wine and provided accommodation. While this was basically true, and was even reinforced by legislation at times, it is a major oversimplification. The original medieval alehouses were mainly private kitchens that chose to supply drink around harvest time when grain was available. During the Tudor period the Crown found it convenient to raise money by selling wine licences to anybody that wanted them, outside the restrictions of the Vintners' Company. Thomas Dekker's polemical writings in the middle of the seventeenth century state that just about every house and business in the suburbs of London was selling beer, whatever else its justification was for being there.

The Beer Act of 1830 similarly made it cheaper and easier to sell beer anywhere, mainly as an antidote to the increasing evil of gin shops. Such laws deliberately undermined the traditional outlets. In the 1830 Act it was specifically stated that it was:

> 'for the better supplying of the public with beer in England,' and to provide
> 'greater facilities for the same therof than are at present afforded by licences
> to keepers of inns, alehouses and victualling houses.'

Inevitably this this led to complaints that everybody was now getting drunk on beer. According to the Canon of St Paul's, Sydney Smith:

> The new Beer Bill has begun its operations. Everybody is drunk. Those
> who are not singing are sprawling. The sovereign people are in a beastly
> state.

The result of these efforts was that during many periods of history any private house or business could become a part time beer house or tavern without the appurtenances that we would consider appropriate to such a role. Small alehouses were sometimes encouraged to provide basic accommodation such as a small room with a multiple use bed or even a free floor, thus encroaching on the trade of inns.

INNS

Buildings that we would recognise as inns probably came in with the Romans. The gap between the exit of the Romans in the year 410 and the start of the Christianised Anglo-Saxon kingdoms around 600 is a grey period when much of the urban structure of England broke down. There is a reference to *tabernae* along the roads during Early Saxon times, and Church Canon Law around 750 forbade priests from visiting taverns, so some of the earlier establishments may have survived. King Edgar passed a law in the middle of the tenth century trying to limit the number of alehouses in each village to one, showing that they must then have been a significant part of the scenery. Political stability and the need to travel must have encouraged business for some inns.

The arrival of Christian monasteries during the Anglo-Saxon period widened choice by providing accommodation for pilgrims at the shrines of popular saints who could be guaranteed to cure particular ills. Pilgrimage, in the sense of travelling to holy places for self-fulfilment or the curing of ills, has always been a feature of organised religious systems.

The Ostrich, Colnbrook

16

In England between around 600 and 1540 this took the form of visiting the shrines of saints in cathedrals and abbeys around the country. Once somebody had become the focus of miracles and unofficially canonised, their relics were translated to a shrine which could be controlled by the Church. The earliest English translation was that of St Augustine at Canterbury in 613, although later shrines were set up to saints who had died earlier such as St Alban (died around 300, translated 793) at the Abbey of that name.[7] Paganism was outlawed in the law codes of King Cnut (anglicised as Canute) and people were forbidden from worshipping at ancient sites such as springs, hills and thorn bushes. Cnut, himself a Scandinavian with a pagan ancestry, made an ostentatious pilgrimage to Bury St Edmunds (then Beodricesworth) in 1020, where he founded an Abbey to reinforce his position as a Christian monarch. This may have been the start of mass pilgrimage in England.

Shrines became a major source of income for the abbeys and cathedrals that contained them, whatever was actually in the casket. The actions of Viking invaders and the occasional irritable monarch meant that martyrs were not in short supply during the Middle Ages. The monastic code drawn up by St Benedict of Nursia around 540 had laid out rules for accommodation and refreshments which were less austere than the earlier habits of the desert fathers. This included provision for pilgrims but they were to be kept separate from the main body of the chapter, with their own buildings and cooking facilities supervised by a delegated brother. Some of these hostels seem to have been privatised as early as the twelfth century. The overflow at popular places like Canterbury and St Albans was quickly taken up by commercial inns that catered for the more well-heeled.

There are a number of surviving pubs, such as the Bingley Arms at Bardsey, the Godbegot in Winchester and the Ostrich at Colnbrook, that have a claim to having started out as monastic hostels in the tenth and eleventh centuries.[8] Many people have proposed that 'Ostrich', which is a rather strange name for a pub, is a corruption of the word 'Hospice' (although others have suggested that it has something to do with feathers). In the late Middle Ages important religious centres like St Albans and Glastonbury could boast of up to a hundred inns each.

Pilgrimages to the Holy Land and the Crusades must have encouraged the mobility of some of the population at various times. This has provided a promotional line for pubs like the Ye Olde Trip to Jerusalem in Nottingham, which boldly asserts that it dates to 1189. This date has been widely rubbished. It is not supported by old records or the age of the existing buildings. However, the associated caves that were dug into the Castle Rock may have provided a convenient place to sleep from earlier times and an even environment for brewing ale. Some have attributed the quality of Nottingham beer to this convenient cellarage. The date chosen is that of the third Crusade, which singularly failed to recapture Jerusalem from the control of the contemporary Arab Muslim sultanate. Christian control was only briefly reinstated in 1229.

The pilgrimage business came to a sudden end between 1536 and 1540 with the dissolution of the monasteries under Henry VIII. However, this did not mean that all the inns just disappeared. A landlord made up a song in 1884 about the fact that there were still ninety-two in St Albans. Some of this survival may have been due to the fact that local Saint's Days were linked to annual fairs and markets which continued to be patronised. The political stability and economic growth of Tudor England encouraged trade and the increased movement of people. In the absence of major public buildings, larger inns also became the main places for court proceedings and for music and the performance of plays.

Ye Olde Trip to Jerusalem, Nottingham

THE PUBLIC HOUSE

The term 'public house' first appeared in the middle of the seventeenth century and became more generally used during the Hanoverian period.[9] The OED is rather ambiguous about it and attributes the first record of the word 'pub' to Hotten's 1859 *Dictionary of Slang*. However, the phrase is found in Tobias Smollett's *The Life and Adventures of Sir Launcelot Greaves*, written in 1760. Interestingly, the place described here seems to have been a real pub, the Black Lion in Weston, Nottinghamshire, and gives us a description of such a business in the eighteenth century:

> It was on the great northern road from York to London, about the beginning of the month of October, and the hour of eight in the evening, that four travellers were by a violent shower of rain driven for shelter into a little public house on the side of the highway, distinguished by a sign which was said to exhibit the figure of a black lion. The kitchen in which they assembled, was the only room for entertainment in the house, paved with red bricks, remarkably clean, furnished with three or four Windsor chairs, adorned with shining plates of pewter and copper sauce pans nicely scoured, that ever dazzled the eyes of the beholder; while a cheerful fire of sea-coal blazed in the chimney.

It was possible to spend the night there but a local suggested they would be better off at an inn a few miles away.

'Public house' described a variety of licensed premises and implied something more professional and permanent than the average alehouse. Most small operators no longer brewed their own ale but bought in beer from breweries and became 'tippling houses'. The focus was on the provider who might move on fairly quickly. Public houses, by contrast, were fixed institutions, often with characteristic names that we would recognise nowadays. They were under the control of licensing magistrates who, at the same time, often tried to suppress tippling houses down back alleys and in cellars. By the first half of the eighteenth century many larger outlets were selling cider, wine and spirits in addition to beer.

One of the main factors in the regularisation of trade was the rise of the commercial breweries. These were increasingly large businesses that needed to control their reputation and finances. One way of doing this was to buy up public houses and ensure that they only sold the brewery's own beer. Landlords, who themselves would not have had the money to buy their own premises, were employed to run them. These 'tied houses' started to appear in earnest after the Napoleonic wars. By the beginning of the nineteenth century many brewers had also started building new, specially designed public houses. The architects of these often included the features of earlier 'gin palaces' with gas lighting, mirrors and comfortable furnishings to produce a more attractive environment. The invention of the bar counter and the beer engine helped to create the public house interior that we are familiar with nowadays.

Legislation from the middle of the nineteenth century effectively eclipsed any lingering official distinctions between alehouses, taverns and inns. It was the public house that was licensed rather than the particulars of what it sold. Nevertheless, there was still a hierarchy of hostelries existing in the popular mind, as in Jerome K. Jerome's *Three Men in a Boat*, published in 1889:

> We therefore decided that we would sleep out on fine nights; and hotel it, and inn it, and pub it, like respectable folks, when it was wet, or when we felt inclined for a change.

The top end of the market had been taken over by French-inspired hotels. The older provincial coaching inns that had catered for stage coaches and the post started to become hotels after the current fashion. The arrival of the railways created entirely different patterns of movement across the country and new hotels in places where they had not existed before. Traditional inns on the old roads had to modify their functions or go out of business. The fact that an old building is now a public house does not tell you much about its earlier history. Most early alehouses were just a house that sold ale and have left little trace in the architectural record. Many small inns, however, would have been specially built and rebuilt in places that traditionally attracted reliable passing trade. Some of these have survived as public houses. When all else failed it was still possible for many centuries to make a reasonable living selling alcohol until the rise of twentieth century supermarket loss-leaders and drink-driving laws. As they lose their trade nowadays these older buildings are not necessarily being demolished any more, but their history is being obscured by being turned into bed and breakfasts, private houses, shops or even Asian restaurants.

INN SIGNS

If you have something to sell it helps to advertise, particularly in northern climes where the activities in a building may not be obvious from the street. Some shops pile their wares up on the side of the road, be they vegetables or cane chairs. This is less practical for alehouses and taverns. An obvious way of advertising is to put up a sign outside in the street.

The American logician and physicist Charles Sanders Peirce claimed to have divided up signs into three logically distinct categories: 'icons', 'indexes' and 'symbols'. Icon comes from the Greek word for 'image' and means a literal representation of something. For instance, a picture or model of a glass or tankard outside a building would be a direct reference to the fact that drink was being sold inside. An index is an image of something that is related to the subject in hand. A picture of a bunch of grapes is not necessarily a suggestion that we have a fruit shop but has generally been understood to indicate the sale of wine. The sign is logically related to the subject, some would say semiotically, but this opens up a whole can of worms that we do not want to go into here. A symbol, by contrast, is an image that has no direct relation to the subject. Its meaning is solely the result of convention. Most people would understand the sign of the Pig and Whistle as referring to a pub (whether fictional or not) but it does not tell you anything about what you can get inside and you certainly would not go there to buy a musical porker. A few claim that such a sign that appears fanciful to us now is actually a corruption of something that was meaningful in the past. A pig might have been a bowl called a 'piggin' or 'pix', with whistle meaning 'wassail' or a word for small change. Even if this were true, the meanings are lost in the modern world and the relationship between pub and sign is seen and understood as arbitrary, as with most pub signs.

Unfortunately, these terms for signs are often used loosely or in other contexts. The issue is muddied even further by psychoanalytic theories that prefer to distinguish between 'signs' which are abstract and 'symbols' which have subconscious meanings attached to them. In the messy world of everyday life, attempts to force such words into academically watertight compartments are not very useful. People grow up in each culture with a set of references that they do not need to think about. For our purpose it is more useful to distinguish between specific signs which are mainly arbitrary labels attached to a particular building and generic signs which inform customers, sometimes indirectly, of the sort of activity that goes on inside. The former has become part of the address of the business whereas the latter, like a pawnbroker's balls or a barber's pole, just tells you what goes on inside. In the past, when many people were illiterate and taxation and postal services were poorly developed, the generic sign was much more useful to everybody.

The pub names we recognise today have developed over the past six hundred years and many can be placed in their historical context. Others may just reflect some prevailing fashion or the whim of a previous owner. It is difficult to be certain how long this naming for its own sake has been going on. In the English Place-Name Survey the earliest reference is to a *taberna de Schyrebourn* in 1280 but this is not really very distinctive. It is only in the last half of the fourteenth century that we have records of names like the George, the New Inn, the Sun and the Tabard.[1] It has been suggested that this sort of naming did not really become universal until the eighteenth century.[2] Some date the origin of the modern English pub sign to the invention of oil painting during the last half of the fifteenth century.

THE EARLY HISTORY OF INN SIGNS

In their *English Inn Signs*, first published in 1866, Jacob Larwood and John Hotten tried to claim such signs may have existed in Rome two thousand years ago. There are a few, brief classical references and archaeological survivals that show the Romans had paintings in or on their taverns but it is difficult to tell from these whether they were signs in the modern sense.

Original painted objects that had been captured as booty in wars were given to the state and exhibited in the Forum or in front of temples. Some of these were copied to decorate the outside of buildings. One supposed piece of evidence that there was a picture of a Cock on a sign in the Forum seems to have resulted from mistranslation of a personal name, Gallus (also *gallus*, the Latin for cockerel), combined with a story about a shield exhibited as a trophy showing a caricature of a Gaul (one of the tribe of the *Galli*) with his tongue sticking out that had been captured by Gaius Marius in his victory over the Cimbrians in BC 101.

In a version of Aesop's fable about the Mice and the Weasels by Phaedrus (around AD 10) he says that this story is seen painted on taverns:

cum victi mures mustelarum exercitu, historia quot sunt in tabernis pingitur,

but this is a general statement and does not necessarily mean that there were taverns called the Mice and Weasels. Excavations show that many, if not most, taverns and inns had paintings, inscriptions and graffiti on the walls but very few of these can be interpreted as a sign that named the building. They were there for decoration or to amuse the customers. For instance, a surviving building that was either a wine bar or a public lavatory in Ostia has paintings of famous Greek philosophers on the wall, two of which have the inscriptions:

'Solon rubbed his stomach to ease his motions', and

'Thales advised determined effort as a cure for constipation.'[3]

However, there was an inn in Pompeii that had a painting on the outside showing an elephant wound up in the coils of a serpent and being defended by a pigmy. Next to it was an inscription that said 'Sittius restored the elephant'.[4] It is not clear whether this refers to the restoration of the building or the painting, and as it has now disappeared all we have to rely on are modern references. It was not unusual for the painters of election notices or adverts to sign their name to them. A district of Rome on the Esquiline Hill was called the *Vicus Ursi Pileati*, which means the 'Quarter of the Bear with a Felt Hat'. It has been suggested by several writers that this name came from a tavern sign in the area but the only evidence put forward for this is that in recent history there has been as an establishment called the Inn of the Bear in a similar position.

Other names have been suggested for taverns of the period, such as the Camel, the Great Eagle, the Little Eagle, the Serpent, the Great Crane, the Sword, the Wheel and the Olives.[5] These have been based on references to a wall painting in the classical literature or images found on walls at excavated sites. In the main street of Herculaneum there are the remains of what has been described as a wine

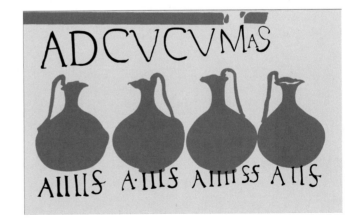

'At the Bowls' in Herculaneum, showing the prices of different wines

shop with a sign showing a row of ewers and above them the large message *Ad Cucumas*. One translation of this has been 'At the Sign of the Bowls'. A *cucuma* was a large cooking pot or kettle, so a more exact translation would be 'At the Cooking Pots'. Whether people would have used such a name to refer to the place is debatable. It looks more like an extended generic sign informing people of the produce on sale, which would have been food as well as wine. Underneath each wine jar is a price for the variety displayed.

Playwrights have always been keen on including drinking dens in their scenarios, as we know from Shakespeare's history plays. References to inns and taverns appear quite frequently in Latin plays from the time of Plautus onwards but nobody says anything like "See you at the Elephant" etc., which would conclusively prove that these paintings were used as names. In Plautus' *Pseudolus* (produced in BC 191 but probably based on a Greek play of a hundred years earlier) one of the chief characters says that he can be found at the third tavern from the city gate belonging to a horizontally challenged old woman called Chrysis.

In the modern world the name of a hotel or pub is part of its address and legal identity. In ancient Greece and Rome these labels did not exist. Places were found by reference to their proximity to local features such as a fountain, a statue, a temple or perhaps sometimes a painting on a wall. In his book on agriculture, Varro gave his maternal aunt's address as at the twenty-fourth milestone from Rome along the Via Salaria.

Around BC 65 the girlfriend of the Roman poet Catullus ran off to live with a Spaniard who owned a local tavern in Rome. In response, Catullus wrote a short, vituperative and fairly obscene poem (XXXVII) in which he identified the Spaniard by name, Egnatius, but could only describe the tavern by its position near the Temple of Castor and Pollux (distinguished by their traditional headgear):

> *Salax taberna uosque contubernales*
> *a pilleatis nona fratribus pila,*

> Lewd tavern and your inmates,
> at the ninth pillar from the felt hatted brothers.

The tavern itself did not seem to have a name. After condemning the sexual habits of the customers he then threatened to draw pictures of his genitalia all over the front of the building. The Temple of Castor and Pollux in Rome was a well-known building in the Forum which had been around for at least four centuries by that date and was part of the foundation mythology of the City, whereas taverns, presumably, came and went.

If you were looking for a building in Rome or Pompeii, having arrived in the general area using street names and prominent landmarks, you would then ask a local where a particular person lived. This seems to have been the principle by which many inns and taverns were identified. In Pompeii, one upmarket inn bears the name of Hyginius Firmus:

> *Hospitium Hyginii Firmi*

Other such buildings have single names on the walls like Hermes, Amarantus or Salvius which are presumed to be those of the owners. One bar near the amphitheatre had a picture of a phoenix on the wall which was used in advertising as a restorative symbol but the bar itself was known by the name (or pseudonym) of the owner Euxinus. Labels on the wine jars found there were addressed:

> To Euxinus, the innkeeper, at Pompeii, near the Amphitheatre.[6]

The wine jars in the tavern of Amarantus also have his name on them. A commercial hotel in Lyons had pictures of several gods on the wall but also the name of the owner:

> MERCVRIVS HIC LVCREM
> PROMITTIT APOLLO SALVTEM
> SEPTVMANVS HOSTPITIVM
> CVM PRANDIO QVI VENERIT
> MELIVS VTETVR POST
> HOSPES VBI MANEAS PROSPICE
>
> Here Mercury promises wealth
> Apollo health,
> Septumanus hospitality
> Where better to stay
> After a good meal?
> Stranger, be careful where you spend the night.[7]

It has been suggested that this hostelry was called *Ad Mercuriam et Apollinem* but in the late Roman Empire many buildings had images of one god or another on the outside.[8] It is likely, therefore, that most establishments were identified by the name of the present or a previous owner, as is found with many bars in Scotland and Ireland nowadays.

Nevertheless, there would no harm in having a sign outside that informed potential customers, particularly those who could not read, of what was obtainable inside. An inn might just have a sign showing that a welcome was available. Near the Forum in Pompeii there is a sculpted sign for a wine shop which shows two people carrying a heavy amphora. Another had a painting nearby which showed brass drinking vessels and funnels. Such generic signs were common in the Roman world. Sculptured reliefs showing people loading barrels to or from carts and ships were quite common across the late Roman empire as far north as Trier in Germany.

 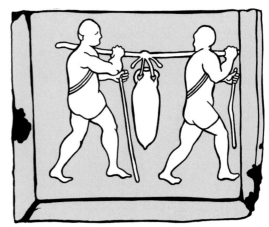

Two Roman signs. On the left an inn sign from Aesernia in Samnium; on the right a sculpted relief from Pompeii showing two slaves carrying a wine amphora

Taverns and bars could also rely on the extensive symbolism surrounding the Greek god Dionysos. Dionysos was a multi-faceted god who collected symbols like hedgehogs collect fleas. People wrote poems about him that listed many of his names and epithets, sometimes amounting to more than a hundred. Only a minority of these were associated with wine, although the Greeks claimed that he had invented it. This was one of the main aspects of his character that was passed on to his Roman successors, Bacchus and Liber. Their most recognisable symbols included vine branches, ivy leaves, bunches of grapes, drinking cups and panthers (sometimes spotted). A painting prised from the column of a tavern on the Street of Dried Fruits (a modern name) in Pompeii shows most of these with Bacchus himself squeezing grapes into a jar accompanied by one of his panthers. Dionysian symbols also extended to pictures of cockerels, hares, foxes, goats and asses, although these had more of a sexual connotation.

Pictures of grapes and vine leaves can be seen on buildings in Pompeii and Herculaneum but one of the more distinctive customs was the Dionysian tradition of hanging up a sprig of ivy or a branch of fresh leaves to show that wine was for sale. This has left us an often repeated quote which has been passed down from a collection of sayings by the first century BC Roman actor Publilius Syrus:

Vino vendibili suspensa hedera non opus est.

There is no need to hang up ivy for wine that you can sell.

The saying has been adapted into English as 'good wine needs no bush', an expression familiar to Shakespeare as it appears in the Epilogue to *As You Like It*:

If it be true that good wine needs no bush,
   'tis true that a good play needs no epilogue
Yet to good wine they do use good bushes;
   and good plays prove better by the help of good epilogues.

A wall painting from Pompeii showing the God Bacchus creating wine

27

ENGLISH INN SIGNS FROM THE MIDDLE AGES ONWARDS

An inn that may be depicted in the Bayeux Tapestry

Some claim to see such a bush or branch in one of the illustrations in the Bayeux tapestry. However, in the Middle Ages the sign had often been transformed into a circular garland or wreath hanging on a pole outside the inn. In England during the fourteenth and fifteenth centuries, inns were sometimes distinguished by adding a form to such a garland, colloquially called a 'hoop'. Thus we have such names as The George on the Hoop, Le Cock in the Hoope, At Checker of the Hope, The Belle on the Hoop.[9] Other explanations of this terminology are that the hoop was the end of a barrel with a picture painted on it or that it was a heraldic expression meaning 'contained within', but the circular support for a garland seem more likely. These might just be descriptions that were written down by local bureaucrats who wanted to keep a record of who was doing what and whether it was legal or not. They are descriptions of the sign rather than the names necessarily used by local patrons.

It has been claimed that the garland in particular was originally made out of hop flowers to show that beer was available rather than ale. In this view there was a hierarchy of signs with a pole or broom for ale, a bush for wine and a garland for beer. That this was partly true is shown by lines in William Winstanley's *Poor Robin's Perambulations from Saffron Walden to London* of 1678:

> This Cheshunt Town is three miles long or near,
> And scattered with houses here and there;
> Some Alehouses upon the Road I saw,
> And some with bushes, showing they Wine did draw,
> But whether Beer or Wine were good or bad
> To test thereof no time I had.

As already noted, there may have been a need to display a hoop because originally the addition of hops to brewing in England was often regarded as an adulteration of ale with 'a wicked and pernicious weed.'[10] Pressure to sell the new European beer came from the fact that it could be stored for much longer and was available at times of year when ale quickly deteriorated. It could also be produced in bulk by independent brewers and transported.

Compared with wine and beer, ale was a more downmarket commodity produced locally as and when grain was available. In the English Middle Ages the sign that it was being offered for sale was the 'ale-stake', a branch or besom hung outside the ale-wife's residence. This may have been a development of the wine bush but by the fourteenth century, it had become a legal requirement for ale. The Assize of Bread and Ale brought in by Henry III in 1266 set out standards for price throughout the country by linking the charge for ale to the price of corn. By the middle of the fourteenth century officials called 'ale-conners' were charged with enforcing the regulations, an onerous position with its own occupational hazards, as described by an anonymous late sixteenth century imitator of Chaucer in *The Cobler of Canterburie*:

Squint eyed was he, and his head
Was bad hued, bloud red
A nose he had that gan show
What liquor he loued I trow
For he had before long seven yeare
Beene of the towne the Ale conner,
His face was ful of pretious stone
Richer in Indie was neuer none
For Rubie, Pearle, and Crysolite
With them all his face was dight,
From the brow to the very chin
Yet to drink he would nere lin:
But swinked with all his might,
At every house where he did sit.

Above:
a woodcut of
a fourteenth
century French
inn

Below:
an English
ale-stake from
the fourteenth
century
Smithfield
Decretals

29

The ale-stake displayed outside premises became a universal requirement in a decree of Richard II in 1393 and showed that the conner's jurisdiction was required.[11] It has been said that one method of assuring the quality of ale needed the use of leather britches. The conner poured some ale on a stool, sat on it for half an hour and then noted whether the stool stuck to his seat, showing that there was still unconverted sugar present and that brewing was not complete. In 1419 in the City of London it was ordained that ale-stakes should not extend more than 7ft into the street. Ale-stakes were not just an English contrivance. They also existed in Germany at *eine Besenwirtschaft*, 'a broom-pub'.[12] The ale-stake could also be garlanded as is suggested by a reference in the Prologue to Chaucer's *Canterbury Tales*:

> A SOMONOUR was ther with us in that place,
> That hadde a fyr-reed cherubynnes face
> A gerland hadde he set upon his heed
> As greet as it were for an ale-stake;

Another way of identifying alehouses in the Middle Ages was from a wooden lattice over the lower windows. We know from later tradition that this was usually painted red. The lattice may have been used as an alternative to ale-stakes before painted signs became more common. A passage in *English Villanies Discovered by Lanthorne and Candle-light* by Thomas Dekker from 1608 describes parts of London:

> But now for all this Act and for all the other Statutes for the same purpose established since, how many parishes in England, how many in and about London, especially throughout the suburbs, do like islands swim, as it were in hot waters, strong Beere, and headstrong Ale.
>
> For to such a height is this sin of drunkenness grown that Cobblers, Tinkers, Pedlars, Porters, all Trades, all Professions sit tippling all day, all night, singing, dancing (when they can stand) laughing, cursing, swearing, fighting.
>
> A whole street is in some places but a continued Ale-house : Not a Shop to be seen between a Red Lattice and a Red Lattice, no workers but all drinkers, not a Trades-man at his occupation, for every Trades-man keeps in that place an Ale-house.
>
> It is an easier life, a lazier life, a trade more gainful : No such comings in as those of the Tap : insomuch that in most of the suburban outroads the best men there that command the rest (the Grand Signiors of the Parish)

as Constables, Head boroughs, and other Officers, are common Ale-house keepers : and he that can lay in many Gayles of Beere, and be furnished with the strongest Ale, and headiest Liquor, carries the Bucklers away from all his fellows.

Looking behind Dekker's hypermoralising (the suburbs contained 'more Ale-houses than there are Taverns in All Spain and France'), it is clear that most of these were not Ale-houses but Houses that sold Ale and Beere in addition to their proper purpose. Like the old Ale-wives they needed some kind of easily attachable sign to show what was also for sale at the moment.

Part of the carving on an early fifteenth century wooden chest showing a scene from Chaucer's Pardoner's Tale. This emphasises the different kinds of windows to be found upstairs and at ground level in a drinking establishment

BARS AND STARS

In Germany and the Low Countries a common sign for a tavern or inn selling drink has always been a pot or *Krug* hanging outside the door. This can be seen in numerous paintings, in particular *The Census at Bethlehem* by Pieter Bruegel the Elder of 1566. This shows a pot hanging by the door and a double garland hanging from a pole. There is also a painted sign on the wall but this is of the double headed Habsburg eagle showing that the inn is being use as a tax office. In fact, the painting has less to do with the New Testament and more with the contemporary level of taxation under Spanish rule which led to the Dutch rebellion a few years later. The large barrel hanging under the eaves is probably a beehive or a dovecot.

The inn and tax office in Pieter Bruegel's The Census at Bethlehem

The practical explanation put forward for the lattice as a sign is that alehouses had to have good ventilation with a trellis giving customers some degree of privacy.[13] This, however, does not explain why they were painted red or why they should appear outside premises that originally had another purpose. The upright hash character was also sometimes used as a symbol for alcohol in alchemy.[14] Whether there was any connection between this and brewing can only be speculated on, and, even if there was, which direction the connection took is unknown. A grid or gate symbol, a *Bierzeiger* (beer indicator) was used as a tapping sign by brewers in Germany as far back as the fourteenth century. This gate symbol may have changed into a hexagram or six-pointed star at some time in the Middle Ages.[15]

In part of his autobiography *Dichtung und Warheit* (Poetry and Meaning) Goethe describes an incident during the 1770s when he was on a local tour of the German countryside with two companions. One of them, who had been annoying everybody by holding forth on his strong anti-Trinitarian beliefs, was thirsty and wanted to stop for a beer at an inn they were passing. As a joke Goethe ordered the coachman to carry on and explained to his friend that they could not stop there because of the beer sign that was outside:

Luckily you didn't see the beer sign! It's composed of two crossed triangles.

With his anti-religious views the sight of one triangle with three sides would have angered him; two triangles would probably have sent him mad. This sign was a *Bierstern* (beer star), also known as a *Brauerstern* (brewer's star). Brewing was strictly regulated in Germany. Beer could only be sold by brewers who also had a licence to tap. In Nuremberg in the sixteenth century a red or white six-pointed star had to be displayed to show that beer was available.[16] The same star became a brewer's guild symbol and was later used as a general symbol for beer across most of southern Germany. It is still to be seen under the name of a *Bierzoigl* in eastern Bavaria where beer is brewed on the premises.

Two explanations have been put forward for the meaning of the *Bierstern*. One is that it is an old alchemy symbol for alcohol that unites the two triangles for fire and water. These were two of the four elements that were central to ancient Greek science. Against this it has been argued that the star was only used in southern Germany and early German brewers would not have been educated enough to know any alchemy. Monasteries played a large role in early brewing and would have excluded a symbol that might have had connections with witchcraft and Judaism. The alternative proposal is that it was a protective symbol, chiefly against fire which was a common hazard in breweries. Comparisons have also been made with the red gridiron that was the symbol for St Lawrence who was barbecued by the Romans.[17]

We can conclude that generic signs for the sale of alcohol in alehouses and taverns were normal across most of Europe from Roman times up until at least the seventeenth century. The details of the evolution of these over the centuries are difficult to describe because the evidence consists of a just a few isolated references and images. Legislation in the early part of the nineteenth century created what we now recognise as the English Public House, which was able to sell all forms of drink in the one establishment. This made generic signs redundant. It may be that sometimes generic symbols, such the Star, the Bush and the Gridiron, passed on from the generic to the specific in a few cases, much like a 'smith' or a 'fletcher' became Smith and Fletcher. The main distinction that has remained is between public houses that just sell drink, and hotels, the Frenchified descendant of the inn, which also provide accommodation.

A modern Bierzoigl from the Oberpfalz, Bavaria

SEVEN STARS

The Seven Stars is a not uncommon name for English public houses and inns. In 2000 there were at least eighty-one with a particular concentration in the West Midlands and the south-west. The recent disturbing attrition rate for pubs means that some of these have already closed down. All the indications are that it is an old name for inns and taverns and was used much more commonly in the past than it is now. Obviously pubs and hotels alter over the years as they are developed, expanded and rebuilt. For instance, the Seven Stars in Brighton claims to have first been granted a licence in 1535 but now looks more like a nineteenth century French chateau on top of a Victorian gin palace. Sometimes the name and sign are changed at the whim of a new owner. However, those who use antiquity as a selling point to attract customers are likely to be motivated to keep as many old features as possible, especially the name. Since the eighteenth century some have even added significant prefixes such as 'Ye Olde' or 'The Original' to make sure there was no confusion.

The antiquity and longevity of the name is in no doubt. A Seven Stars in Lombard Street in the City of London appeared in a list of brewers from 1420, a parish register of 1424 and a survey from 1708.[2] The archives of the City of Bristol have records of licensing returns between 1752 and 1764. These show that during this period there were nine inns or alehouses called the Seven Stars in the city. Only one of these has survived.[3]

The antiquity of some surviving Seven Stars is suggested by the fact that they are on roads that appear to have been named after the pub. Both the Seven Stars in Dinton, Buckinghamshire, and the Seven Stars in Tamerton Foliot, Devon, are on roads called Seven Stars Lane. John Roque's 1746 map of London has three Seven Stars Alleys and two Seven Stars Courts on it. The only one of these Seven Stars that can be directly related to a building was next to St Dunstan's Church off Fleet Street, although the reference books tell us this was a toyshop! In their *History of Signboards,* Larwood and Hotton recorded only four public houses called the Seven Stars in London in 1864. However, Bryant Lillywhite's compendious *London Signs* lists fifty-one premises claiming use of the sign between 1420 and 1853.

The evidence for many of Lillywhite's Seven Stars is second hand at best, and only about a fifth can be confidently linked to actual taverns. Around half of them were recognised from farthing and halfpenny trade tokens that they issued between 1648 and 1660 when small change was in short supply. These copper or brass tokens were used by a variety of businesses in England but more than a thousand different kinds are said to have come from purveyors of drink in one form or another. Writing in 1697 in his

*Opposite:
The various interpretations of the Seven Stars sign*[1]

Numismata, the diarist John Evelyn described them as:

The tokens which every taverne and tippling house (in the days of the late Anarchy among us) presum'd to stamp for immediate exchange.

Other businesses issued tokens as well. These can be recognised by their trademarks or guild arms, suggesting that the signs on tokens were not turned out at random but were chosen to reflect the goods on offer. Therefore it comes as a surprise when Lillywhite says that three of these Seven Star tokens came from goldsmiths, two from haberdashers, two mercers, two booksellers, and the rest included a hosier, a stay maker, a coffee house, a banker, a cabinet maker, a potter, a printer, a scrivener, a milliner and a toy shop.

Questions have to be raised as to why such a disparate collection of businesses should have chosen this sign and what use it could have been to them. When we are told that a token inscribed:

ROBERT HOLLIS AT YE SEVEN STARRS IN HOVNS DITCH HIS HALF PENNY

may have been issued by a scrivener we have to express reservations. There is no clear reason why the Seven Stars should have had anything to do with scriveners, even less to imply that it might be 'Ye Olde Scrivener'. The name suggests some antiquity which has become normal for pubs but seems unlikely for other businesses. Nevertheless, tying the name to a particular type of hostelry can also be difficult. For instance, the Seven Stars in Henley-on-Thames is thought to have been a large, flourishing inn in the seventeenth century before declining to become a small beer house. It was last reported as trading as a pub in 1751 and sometime after that the building was demolished.[4]

If a token says 'At the Seven Stars' then we may reasonably conclude that there was a fixed sign to go with it and that it was there for a reason, although, significantly, these tokens had to have the name or initials of the issuer on them as well. With this sort of ambiguity it would be comforting if we could find a Seven Stars which produced a token in the seventeenth century that still exists as a pub. Fortunately, we have a farthing token which says:

HENRY. PENIELL. AT. YE. SEVEN. STARS. IN. FALMOUTH. 1666.

There is still a venerable bar in Falmouth with this name which is known to have been licensed since the seventeenth century. Even so, bearing Evelyn's observations in mind, some of these premises may have been tippling houses, buildings which were not inns or taverns in any meaningful way but which just sold drink and wanted to advertise it. The fact that they may also have been scriveners, goldsmiths, toyshops or anything else could be irrelevant.

The Seven Stars, Falmouth in its modern guise

The distribution of modern Seven Stars public houses and hotels (left) and those claiming an ancestry to between the fourteenth and seventeenth centuries (right)

The problem of discovering the origin and meaning of the name Seven Stars then becomes one of deciding what these seven stars were and how they may have become associated with some part of the drinks trade. For this we need to look at the history and distribution of the name. As noted above, modern pubs and hotels called the Seven Stars show a concentration in the south and west of England. There is some leakage into Wales and the north-east but if we separate out those premises that have a reasonable claim to antiquity the spread becomes much more restricted. They are confined to the south of England below the Thames, across to Devon and Cornwall, and spread up into the West Midlands to south Lancashire. None are found in East Anglia, the eastern Midlands or the north-east. There seems no reason to believe that there is anything natural or geographical about this pattern. Any explanation for the name has to take this peculiar distribution into account. It is an understanding of the cultural and political history of these areas which will ultimately tell us what the sign of the Seven Stars really means.

MANCHESTER

At the end of the nineteenth century, Ye Olde Seven Stars on Withy Grove in Manchester claimed to be the oldest licensed premises in Great Britain. It was first photographed in 1877. During the boom in the postcard industry before World War I, numerous photos of the exterior (and rarer ones of the interior) were published which are still available to collectors. Two views are reproduced here, one of which shows the large metal hanging sign with just the ring of seven stars and no name. Unfortunately the building is no longer with us, having fallen foul of road-widening efforts at the beginning of the twentieth century. It was emptied of its contents in 1907 and demolished in 1911. 'Relics' from the premises were auctioned off and fetched nearly a £1,000, a more impressive sum then than it would be now. They included a 400-year old oak table, the doors of the New Bailey Prison, Salford, a 200-year old clock, a man trap and, presumably, 'the cupboard that has never been opened in living memory'. Anything that may have been left of the inn itself has long been buried under one of the incarnations of the Arndale Shopping Centre.

Its loss did not go without comment at the time. A letter to the *Manchester City News* of 18th March 1911 said:

> The lease of one of the few old buildings in the city expires shortly, and it is feared the quaint old hostelry full of memories of a past and gone Manchester will disappear about the same time. Romance lurks in the nooks and corners of the old inn and legend encrusts its history, while its characteristic features – black and white front, big black gable, low ceilinged rooms and small-paned windows have attested its antiquity.

Most of what we know about the place is to be found in Charles Harper's 1906 edition of *The Old Inns of England*. As a reasonably sceptical eye-witness it is worth giving his account here.[5]

> Our next claimant in the way of antiquity is the "Seven Stars" inn at Manchester, a place little dreamt of, in such a connection, by most people; for, although Manchester is an ancient city, it is so modernised in general appearance that it is a place wherein the connoisseur of old-world inns would scarce think of looking for examples. Yet it contains three remarkably picturesque old taverns, and the neighbouring town of Salford, nearly as much a part of Manchester as Southwark is of London, possesses

Ye Olde Seven Starrs Hotel, Withy Grove, Manchester
The oldest licensed house in Great Britain

another. To take the merely picturesque, unstoried houses first: these are the "Bull's Head," Greengate, Salford; the "Wellington" inn, in the Market-place, Manchester; the tottering, crazy-looking tavern called "Ye Olde Rover's Return," on Shude Hill, claiming to be the "oldest beer-house in the city," and additionally said once to have been an old farmhouse "where the Cow was kept that supplied Milk to The Men who built the 'Seven Stars,' " and lastly - but most important - the famous "Seven Stars" itself, in Withy Grove, proudly bearing on its front the statement that it has been licensed over 560 years, and is the oldest licensed house in Great Britain.

The "Seven Stars" is of the same peculiar old-world construction as the other houses just enumerated, and is just a humble survival of the ancient rural method of building in this district: with a stout framing of oak timbers and a filling of rag-stone, brick and plaster. Doubtless all Manchester, of the period to which these survivals belong, was of like architecture. It was a method of construction in essence identical with the building of modern steel-frame houses and offices in England and America: modern construction being only on a larger scale. In either period, the framework of wood or of metal is set up first and then clothed with its architectural features, whether of stone, brick, or plaster. The "Seven Stars," however, is no skyscraper. So far from soaring, it is of only two floors, and, placed as it is — sandwiched as it is, one might say — between grim, towering blocks of warehouses, looks peculiarly insignificant.

We may suppose the existing house to have been built somewhere about 1500, although there is nothing in its rude walls and rough axe-hewn timbers to fix the period to a century more or less. At any rate, it is not the original "Seven Stars" on this spot, known to have been first licensed in 1356, three years after inns and alehouses were enquired into and regulated, under Edward the Third; by virtue of which record, duly attested by the archives of the County Palatine of Lancaster, the present building claims to be the "oldest Licensed House in Great Britain."

There is a great deal of very fine, unreliable "history" about the "Seven Stars," and some others, but it is quite true that the inn is older than Manchester Cathedral, for that — originally the Collegiate Church — was not founded until 1422; and topers with consciences remaining to them may lay the flattering unction to their souls that, if they pour libations here, in the Temple of Bacchus, rather than praying at the Cathedral, they do, at any rate (if there be any virtue in that), frequent a place of greater antiquity.

Opposite: Two postcard views of the Seven Stars, Withy Grove Manchester, that were issued around 1900. The lower one shows the independent hanging sign of the stars in the original rosette form

And antiquity is cultivated with care and considerable success at the "Seven Stars," as a business asset. The house issues a set of seven picture-postcards, showing its various "historic" nooks and corners, and the leaded window-casements have even been artfully painted, in an effort to make the small panes look smaller than they really are; while the unwary visitor in the low-ceilinged rooms falls over and trips up against all manner of unexpected steps up and steps down.

It is, of course, not to be supposed that a house with so long a past should be without its legends, and in the cellars the credulous and uncritical stranger is shown an archway that, he is told, led to old Ordsall Hall and the Collegiate Church! What secret and thirsty souls they must have been in that old establishment! But the secret passage is blocked up now. Here we may profitably meditate awhile on those "secret passages" that have no secrets and afford no passage; and may at the same time stop to admire the open conduct of that clergyman who, despising such underground things, was accustomed in 1571, according to the records of the Court Leet, to step publicly across the way in his surplus, in sermon-time, for a refreshing drink.

"What stories this old Inn could recount if it had the power of language!" exclaims the leaflet sold at the "Seven Stars" itself. The reflection is sufficiently trite and obvious. What stories could not any building tell, if it were so gifted? But fortunately, although walls metaphorically have ears, they have not – even in literary imagery – got tongues, and so cannot blab. And well too, for if they could and did, what a cloud of witness there would be, to be sure. Not an one of us would get a hearing, and not a soul be safe.

But what stories, in more than one sense, Harrison Ainsworth told![6] He told a tale of Guy Fawkes, in which that hero of the mask, the dark-lantern and the powder-barrel escaped, and made his way to the "Seven Stars," to be concealed in a room now called "Ye Guy Fawkes Chamber." Ye gods!

We know perfectly well that he did not escape, and so was not concealed in a house to which he could not come, but – well, there! Such fantastic tales, adopted by the house, naturally bring suspicion upon all else; and the story of the horse-shoe upon one of its wooden posts is therefore, rightly or wrongly, suspect. This is a legend that tells how, in 1805, when we were at war with Napoleon, the Press Gang was billeted at the "Seven Stars," and seized a farmer's servant who was leading a horse with a cast shoe along Withy Grove. The Press Gang could not legally press a farm-servant, but that probably mattered little, and he was led away; but, before he went, he nailed the cast horse-shoe to a post, exclaiming, "Let this stay till I come from the wars to claim it!" He never returned, and the horse-shoe remains in place to this day.

The room adjoining the Bar parlour is called nowadays the "Vestry." It was, according to legends, the meeting-place of the Watch, in the old days before the era of police; and there they not only met but stayed, the captain ever and again rising, with the words, "Now we will have another glass, and then go our rounds"; upon which, emptying their glasses, they all would walk round the tables and then re-seat themselves.

A great deal of old Jacobean and other furniture has been collected, to fill the rooms of the "Seven Stars," and in the "Vestry" is the "cupboard that has never been opened" within the memory of a living man. It is evidently not suspected of holding untold gold. Relics from the New Bailey Prison, demolished in 1872, are housed here, including the doors of the condemned cell, and sundry leg irons; and genuine Carolean and Cromwellian tables are shown. The poet who wrote of some marvelously omniscient personage –

> And still the wonder grew
> That one small head could carry all he knew,

would have rejoiced to know the "Seven Stars," and might have been moved to write a similar couplet, on how much so small a house could be made to hold.

As Charles Harper tells us, the Seven Stars relentlessly promoted its own mythology through advertisements, booklets and postcards (although this seems to have had little influence on the owners who closed it down). According to a printed notice on a sideboard next to way in, the seven remarkable features of the establishment were:

YE TRADITIONAL ROOMS
YE GUY FAWKS CHAMBER
YE VESTRIE
YE CLOISTER
THE OLD SILVER PLATE CAN BE SEEN IN THE BAR
THE HORSE SHOE AT THE FOOT OF THE STAIRS
AT THE TOP OF THE STAIRS STANDS AN OLD CLOCK 200 YEARS OLD

This room is in excellent preservation and contains a handsome Oak Settle dated 1728, also a superb Chair, on which is inscribed the name of Richard Lumley, Viscount Lumley of Waterford. This nobleman was the ancestor of the present Earl of Scarborough, and the chair bears the family arms, crest, and motto: "Murus aenus consientia sona" (A sound conscience is a wall of brass) In the centre of the back a fine piece of carving represents Balliol, King of Scotland, taking the oath of allegiance to Edward I.

THE BAR PARLOUR. "Ye Olde Seven Stars," Manchester   *E. T. & Co., Copyright*
(The oldest Licensed House in Great Britain)

One of the seven postcards issued by the Seven Stars showing part of the parlour and the service area

The seven postcards mainly showed views of the sitting rooms, including the 'Guy Faux Chamber', and a photo of the cellar with a blocked off passage way.

There were several signs outside the Seven Stars. The painted signs on the wall were obviously the most recent since they had adverts on them for the antiquity of the building. This suggests that the hanging sign of seven stars with no name attached to it (most easily seen in the colour postcard image) was the oldest. Exactly how old is impossible to say as any sign suffers wear and tear from the elements and needs to be replaced at some point. A number of postcards show the metal armature in place but without the sign hanging from it (although this may have been shortly before demolition). It was clearly a circle of six stars with a seventh in the middle.

The painted signs that were visible in the first decade of the twentieth century advertise the purported date of the inn's first licence. One, proclaiming that it was 'Ye Olde Seven Starrs', said that it had been licensed for over 550 years and another had 540 years. The latter appears newer and had been repainted from the 1877 photograph which shows no dates. Harper's drawing of the front only shows the first board with a date of 560 years. If we add 560 to 1356 we arrive at 1916, long after Harper and the various photographers and post-card senders had moved on, so there are grounds for confusion in all of these dates.

A Palatinate was an independent Duchy that could administer its own laws and taxes separately from the royal courts. The Duchy of Lancaster was created in 1351 under Henry de Grosmont in the reign of Edward III. Many of its legal documents survive in a remarkably well preserved state and are now in the National Archives in Kew after having spent most of their life in Lancaster Castle. The Duchy court was based in Preston and met twice a year. There is a complete series of rolls from 1351 up until the death of Duke Henry in 1361. The powers then went into abeyance until 1377 when they were renewed under John of Gaunt. The most relevant document for our purposes is 30 Edw III (6 Duke Hen) for 1356, now known as DL 35/5. Unfortunately, to extract anything out of this you need to be expert in Medieval Latin, medieval law and, even worse, medieval handwriting, so the exact legal status and date of the early Seven Stars remains open to investigation.

The inn is probably visible at the junction of Withy Grove and Shude Hill on a map of Manchester that was drawn around 1650. A report in the *Manchester City News* of 1885 says that during alterations that were being carried out some silver plate from the era of the Civil War was found. This was thought to be the mess plate of a regiment of royalist dragoons who had stayed there and hidden it as the result of some kind of emergency.

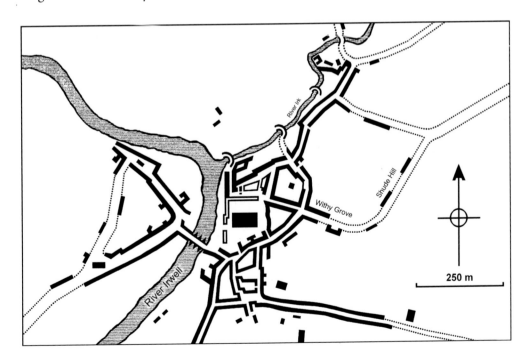

Manchester around the year 1650

One of the original reasons for setting up the Duchy of Lancaster was to provide a northern bulwark against Scottish invasions. The only time that this actually became an issue was in in the eighteenth century when Bonnie Prince Charlie turned up on the doorstep during his abortive mission to take back the crowns of England and Scotland for the Stuarts. The Jacobites arrived in Manchester on the 29 November 1745. They were hopeful of recruiting supporters there but only 180 signed up out of population of 40,000. The next day they left for Derby. Here they decided that 4,500 men were not enough to capture London and were led to believe that reinforcements (largely fictional) had arrived in Scotland from France. They resolved to go back to Scotland and stayed the night again in Manchester on 9 December. According to the Manchester Leet Court Records for 11 December 1745, John Hulme of the Seven Stars was paid 5s 6d for the hire of horses to take word south that the Highlanders had just marched through town. This so far remains the main surviving mention of the inn in the historical record. Charles Edward Stuart himself stayed in the Wellington Inn, but some of his entourage may have bedded elsewhere. His Highland Volunteers were presumably more used to sleeping on the ground, although court records from the sixteenth century suggest that at this time there were around thirty alehouses and inns in Manchester.

The junction of Withy Grove and Dantzic Street today, part of the last view from Ye Olde Seven Stars

Whatever the reality of the dates put forward for the inn in Manchester, it was clearly an old building, going back to early Tudor times or possibly earlier and we have no reason to believe that it was ever called anything other than the Seven Stars. The sign, six stars in a circle with a seventh in the middle, was the original Seven Stars sign. This was probably a generic sign that was relevant to the period and it is only in the recent past that the Seven Stars has been modified by people to produce other images for their own purposes.

The only Seven Stars in Manchester these days is a Wetherspoons/Lloyds Bar next to Withy Grove in Dantzic Street which has appropriated the name. However, during the nineteenth century there were a number of Seven Stars in and around Manchester which have since disappeared. The Seven Stars on the Oldham Road in Larkhill first appears as a beer house in 1848 but lost its licence in 1870. The site is now a Chinese supermarket. The Seven Stars in York Street was demolished in 1964 to make room for a new ring road. A Seven Stars on the Regent Road, Salford was opened in

1868 as the Military Arms but renamed in 1893. The building was condemned in 1933 and demolished. Another Seven Stars in the village of Clifton was opened in 1786, closed in 1938 and demolished in 1955.

This leaves us with an interesting building on Ashton Old Road near to the new Manchester City football complex. It was recorded as a hotel in 1961 but closed as a pub in 2010. It is now another Chinese supermarket. In style it seems to date from the late nineteenth or early twentieth century and somebody clearly went to some length and expense to establish the brand name and symbolism by having stars and bunches of grapes embedded as reliefs into the outside.

The Seven Stars, Ashton Old Road, Manchester

The outside decoration on the Seven Stars, Ashton Old Road Manchester

EXETER

Another old Seven Stars with a complex history was to be found in Exeter. This first appears in the records during 1657 in the autobiography of George Fox, one of the founders of the Quaker movement:

> We then travelled to Exeter; and at the sign of the Seven Stars, an inn at the bridge foot, had a general meeting of Friends out of Cornwall and Devonshire; to which came Humphrey Lower, Thomas Lower, and John Ellis from the Land's End; Henry Pollexfen, and Friends from Plymouth; Elizabeth Trelawny, and diverse other Friends. A blessed heavenly meeting we had, and the Lord's everlasting power came over all, in which I saw and said that the Lord's power had surrounded this nation round about as with a wall and bulwark, and His seed reached from sea to sea. Friends were established in the everlasting Seed of life, Christ Jesus, their Life, Rock, Teacher, and Shepherd.
>
> Next morning Major Blackmore sent soldiers to apprehend me; but I was gone before they came. As I was riding up the street I saw the officers going down; so the Lord crossed them in their design, and Friends passed away peaceably and quietly. The soldiers examined some Friends after I was gone, asking them what they did there; but when they told them that they were in their inn, and had business in the city, they went away without meddling any further with them.

Notice that they were 'at the sign of the Seven Stars' rather than at a named inn.

In the early eighteenth century theatrical performances could not be put on within the city walls and, since it was the nearest inn outside, the Seven Stars was the venue of choice. As advertised in *Brice's Weekly*, in 1721 and 1725 the audience saw:

> Punch's theatre, with artificial actors, also many wonderful Fancies as dancing with swords by a girl but ten years old, who turns many 100 times around with so swift a motion that it's scarce possible to distinguish her Face from the hinder part of her Head.
>
> Advert, of Punch's Theatre at the 7 Stars St. Thos. Plays by artificial actors also legerdemain & a tumbling girl, 10 years old.

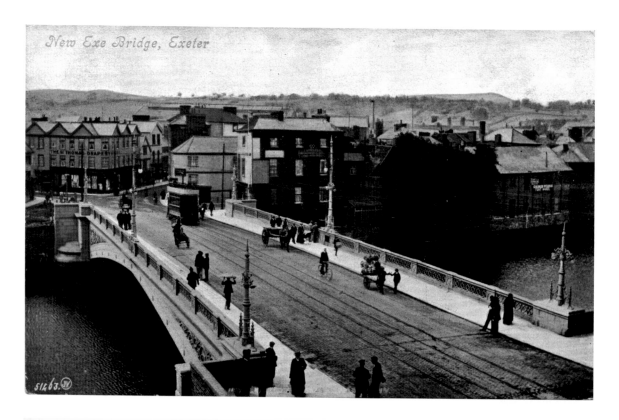

The Duke of Grafton's Company appeared there in 1726 with *The Busie Body* and John Gay produced his *Beggar's Opera* at the Seven Stars in 1728.[7] It is also cited in the Midsummer Sessions of 1726 as having suffered flood damage and appears in a number of eighteenth century engravings and paintings.

Opposite, above: The new tram bridge over the River Exe in 1907 showing the Seven Stars Hotel

Opposite, below: The Exe Bridge and the Seven Stars in 1930

Part of the first map of Exeter drawn by Remigius Hogenberg in 1587 showing the West Gate and the medieval bridge

The original Seven Stars in Exeter was characterised by its position at the western end of the Exe Bridge. Exeter began as a Roman Fort on the first inland crossing point of the River Exe. The Romano-British town of *Isca Dumnoniorum* developed into the medieval walled city. To begin with there was a wooden bridge over the Exe (made of 'Clappers of Tymbre') which had probably been there since Roman times but a stone one was built around 1200. This had to be at least 700 ft. long to cover some marshy ground and part of it can still be seen. Not all of this is original as it consists of a mixture of semi-circular Norman arches and later pointed gothic ones from repairs done in the fifteenth century. The first published map of Exeter which was produced in 1587 shows this bridge outside the city's West Gate. At the western end of the bridge there is an isolated building. Although there is no direct evidence for it this is almost certainly the Seven Stars. Like many inns in England that are just outside city walls, it would have provided accommodation for travellers who had arrived after the gates were shut. The first inn could therefore have been built at any time from the thirteenth century onwards.

The remains of the medieval Exe Bridge

The medieval bridge was partially demolished and replaced with a shorter three-arch version in 1778. The Seven Stars was presumably also modernised into the more substantial Georgian building that is visible in an engraving by John Gendall.[8] By 1905 the Georgian bridge had been replaced by a single span iron bridge that was capable of taking trams. Its opening was the occasion for ceremonies and the publishing of a number of postcards which also include views of the Seven Stars at the height of its commercial success. One of these shows the sign on the wall facing the river as a circle of six stars and a seventh in the middle. In 1933, part of building was demolished for road-widening and by 1940 doubts were being raised about its fitness as a hotel. The problem disappeared in 1943 when the whole area was destroyed by German bombing. Plans had already been started in 1938 to transfer the licence to new premises opposite the cattle market half a mile to the south down the Alphington Road but they were not completed until 1965. This pub had an interesting sign showing a cow's head with seven stars above it, probably a reference to the market opposite but possibly also including some more esoteric symbolism. In 2003 the building was redesigned to become a modern lounge bar and restaurant with no redeeming antiquarian features. The site of the old Seven Stars has disappeared entirely under the modern road system.

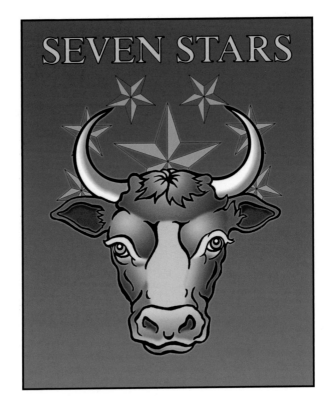

The first sign of the new Seven Stars in Exeter when it was opposite the cattle market

TOTNES

In his *History of the Kings of Britain*, written in 1136, Geoffrey of Monmouth claimed Totnes was the place where the classical hero Brutus of Troy landed after escaping from Virgil's *Æneid* and Homer's *Iliad* so that all English Royalty could trace their descent back to the Trojans via the Roman Empire. Later we are told that the Celtic King Uther Pendragon came back from Brittany and landed in the same place to defend his kingdom from the Saxons. Fantastic as some of these histories may have been it shows that Totnes was considered to be a significant place in the Middle Ages. This was the port where people who had sailed from the Mediterranean and western France were supposed to land.

The modern town probably started as one of the Royal Boroughs that Alfred the Great created to defend Wessex from the Vikings at the beginning of the tenth century. Coins were minted there in the reign of King Edgar (959-75). It owed its prominence to being at the head of the navigable reaches of the River Dart. There may have been a track way and ford there going back to Neolithic times and later a wooden bridge, but the first stone bridge was built around 1210. Over the next fifty years a number of chapels were founded next to the west end of the bridge, the largest of which was to the Anglian King Edmund the Martyr who had been killed by invading Danes in 869.

The Royal Seven Stars in Totnes, Devon

The standard story then becomes that a religious hostel was built next to the chapel, presumably for pilgrims who were travelling abroad, and that this was decorated with the sign of the Seven Stars because this was the emblem of the Virgin Mary. There are a number of problems with this account. Firstly, as we shall see later, the Seven Stars never had anything to do with the Virgin Mary. Secondly, a chapel was not a monastic institution staffed by monks. This one had been built by the local nobility who paid for its upkeep and the support of one priest. There is evidence that before the Wars of the Roses the land belonged to the de la Zouche family. It was confiscated by Henry VII and given to another local baron, Sir Richard Edgcumbe of Cotehele, in 1486. The chantry lands were then leased to the Abbot of Buckfast, who seems to have been a local merchant living in Totnes. A rent was paid to the barony of:

> a pair of golden spurs out of a tenement called the Seven Stars.

References to the rent of 'a pair of golden spurs' are also found in local records from 1562, 1642 and 1680.[9] This suggests that the Seven Stars was a functioning, profitable (particularly if the golden spurs were paid annually) and not very religious business next to the bridge, whatever its association with the chapel may have been, and that it was a commercial inn from its inception. The first record of it actually being called the Seven Stars Inn is in a will of 1675.

The property was leased in 1680 by a local merchant and future mayor of Totnes, George Rooke, who dispensed with the 'tenement', widened the bridge and built a new Seven Stars on the old site. His daughter married a Nicholas Trist of Bowden who became High Sherriff of Devon in 1708. The inn remained in the Trist family for most of the eighteenth century. Although he does not mention the inn by name in his book, *A Tour Thro' the Whole Island of Great Britain,* published in 1724, it is generally considered that Daniel Defoe stayed there in 1720 while undertaking his research work:

> About 22 miles from Excester we go to Totnes on the river Dart. This is a very good town; of some Trade, but has more gentlemen in it than tradesmen of note. They have a very fine stone bridge over the river which being within seven or eight miles of the sea, is very large, and the tide flows 10 or 12 foot at the bridge. Here we had the diversion of seeing them catch fish with the assistance of a dog .... The person who went with us, who was our landlord at a great inn next the bridge, put in a net on a hoop at the end of a pole, the pole going across the hoop. The net being fixed at one end of the place they put in the dog, and he drives all the fish into the net.

The inn became the main stagecoach post between Plymouth and Exeter in the nineteenth century, and a grand staircase and upstairs ballroom were added. This seems to have been the time when it was renamed the Royal Seven Stars, probably as the result of eminent cadets passing through on their way to Plymouth or the Royal Naval College in Dartmouth. William III may also have visited Totnes when he set up the Royal Navy dockyard in Plymouth.

The sign used by the Royal Seven Stars is now a modernised castellated version with two rows of three stars and a seventh on the top. The older sign was based on the arms of Nicholas Trist of Bowden. According to Burke, this was:

Azure, a quarterfoil between an orle of seven estoiles or, a canton-ermine, quarterly.

Estoiles were normally stars with wavy edges. The straight edged golden stars here were often called mullets. This does not refer to a fish or somebody's hairstyle but was a version of the French heraldry term *molette*, meaning the roundel of a spur. The fact that there are seven of them here may be coincidental or the arms may have been based on having a prosperous inn with that name. The five lines and dots in the upper left quarter or canton are the signs for ermine. This is a fur favoured by titled persons which is made out of the skins of northern stoats that turn white in the winter. The end of their tail, however, remains black and furriers kept this when they stitched the pelts together. The ermine sign in heraldry is a conventional representation of this tail.

Left: The arms of Nicholas Trist of Bowden

Right: The modernised sign for the Royal Seven Stars, Totnes

The Seven Stars, Dartmouth

Eight miles down the estuary as the boat sails, is the town of Dartmouth which was used as a sheltered deep water port from the earliest times. Defoe noted that the Dart estuary would be capable of holding 500 ships in comfort. It was also renowned for its pilchards, which were sometimes driven up the river as far as Totnes by schools of porpoises. The local merchants traded with Spain, Portugal, Italy and North America.

The Seven Stars here on Smith Street claims to be the oldest pub in the town. This is in the older centre of Dartmouth and is recorded from the thirteenth century when it may have been the focus of the ship building trades. Unfortunately, as a result of extensive embanking of the seafront, the centre has moved. The Seven Stars has been closed for the last few years. Its exact history is unclear. It may have been formed out of two earlier properties in the eighteenth century. However, as we have seen from Totnes, this does not exclude it from an even earlier existence. Although not originally an inn, the oldest looking pub in Dartmouth is the Cherub on Higher Street. The fact that most of the English forces for the Second and Third Crusades actually left from the Dart estuary means that any of these Devon hostelries could claim to predate the Trip to Jerusalem in Nottingham.

The Cherub,
Dartmouth

BRISTOL

As mentioned above, in the middle of the eighteenth century there were nine Seven Stars in Bristol out of a total of at least 850 inns and alehouses (around one for every fifty inhabitants).[10] Many were concentrated around the harbour. There were four Seven Stars in 1775. Now there is just one. It is a stone-built building which, an architectural historian tells us, has probably always been an inn.[11] Pictures of it have been produced purporting to show an original timber-framed structure. On a narrow cobbled lane opposite the church of St Thomas, it was at one time just to the east of the Sheep Market.

The earliest record of the Seven Stars is from August 1671 when an agreement was drawn up under the will of a John Pope (who may have been a former landlord) by his son for a charge on the house's takings to be used for an annual sermon and a donation to the poor on the first Sunday after All Saints Day. The 'Seven Starrs' was also allowed to have direct access to the Sheep Market. The other parties were 'the feofees of St. Thomas' suggesting that the ground on which the inn was built belonged to the church. The Seven Stars chief claim to fame nowadays, however, is its involvement in the abolition of the slave trade.

The Seven Stars, Bristol

In the middle of the eighteenth century Bristol's wealth as a port was heavily dependent on the slave trade before its dominant position in this business was taken over by Liverpool. Thomas Clarkson who, together with William Wilberforce and Granville Sharp, was one of the prime movers in the abolition of slavery, visited the port in 1787 to collect information for a pamphlet that was to bring notice of the trade to a wider audience. As an ordained minister himself, Clarkson seems to have gravitated to others in the church who could help him and they introduced him to the landlord of the Seven Stars, as he relates in his two-volume history of the abolition of the trade published in 1808.

On my return to Bristol, I determined to inquire into the truth of the reports that seamen had an aversion to enter, and that they were inveigled, if not often forced, into this hateful employment. For this purpose I was introduced to a landlord of the name of Thompson, who kept a public-house called the Seven Stars. He was a very intelligent man, was accustomed to receive sailors, when discharged at the end of their voyages, and to board them till their vessels went out again, or to find them births in others. He avoided however all connection with the Slave-trade, declaring that the credit of his house would be ruined, if he were known to send those, who put themselves under his care, into it.

From him I collected the truth of all that had been stated to me on this subject. But I told him I should not be satisfied until I had beheld those scenes myself, which he had described to me; and I entreated him to take me into them, saying that I would reward him for all his time and trouble, and that I would never forget him while I lived. To this he consented; and as three or four slave-vessels at this time were preparing for their voyages, it was time that we should begin our rounds. At about twelve at night we generally set out, and were employed till two and sometimes three in the morning. He led me from one of those public-houses to another, which the mates of the slave-vessels used to frequent to pick up their hands. These houses were in Marsh-street, and most of them were then kept by Irishmen. The scenes witnessed in these houses were truly distressing to me; and yet, if I wished to know practically what I had purposed, I could not avoid them. Music, dancing, rioting, drunkenness, and profane swearing, were kept up from night to night. The young mariner, if a stranger to the port, and unacquainted with the nature of the Slave-trade, was sure to be picked up. The novelty of the voyages, the superiority of the wages in this over any other trades, and the privileges of various kinds, were set before him. Gulled in this manner he was frequently enticed to the boat, which was waiting to carry him away. If these prospects did not attract him, he was plied with liquor till he became intoxicated, when a bargain was made over him between the landlord and the mate. After this his senses were kept in such a constant state of stupefaction by the liquor, that in time the former might do with him what he pleased. Seamen also were boarded in these houses, who, when the slave-ships were going out, but at no other time, were encouraged to spend more than they had money to pay for; and to these, when they had thus exceeded, but one alternative was given, namely, a slave-vessel, or a gaol. These distressing scenes I found myself obliged frequently to witness, for I was no less than nineteen times occupied in making these hateful rounds. And I can say from my own experience, and all the information I could collect from Thompson and others that no such practices were in use to obtain seamen for other trades.

Thompson, of the Seven Stars, had informed me that Frazer was the only man sailing out of that port for slaves, who had not been guilty of cruelty to his seamen.

I began to perceive in a little time the advantage of having cultivated an acquaintance with Thompson of the Seven Stars. For nothing could now pass in Bristol, relative to the seamen employed in this trade, but it was soon brought to me.

I was very unwilling to refuse any thing to Thompson. I was deeply bound to him in gratitude for the many services he had rendered me, but I scarcely saw how I could serve him on this occasion.[12]

At this time Clarkson seems to have been more concerned with the treatment of the sailors on slave ships which was probably the reason so many were prepared to talk to him. The death rate among crews on these ships was sometimes almost as high as among the slaves that they carried. He intervened a number of times, at no small risk to himself, to bring legal proceedings against some of the more brutal captains. On one occasion he narrowly avoided being thrown off a pier in Liverpool Docks by a group of officers and owners.

It must be remembered that there were no actual slaves in Bristol, other than a very few who might have ended up as seamen. The so called Triangular Trade consisted of sailing from England to Africa with manufactured goods and exchanging them for slaves from the local dealers there. These were then ferried in the Middle Passage to the Americas where (if they were still alive) they were sold to plantations. The ships then loaded up with suitable produce such as sugar, tobacco and rum for the return trip back to Europe.

Under the influence of the Bristol Radical History Group the sign of the Seven Stars in Bristol has been changed to the seven stars of the Plough or Big Dipper. This is presented as the 'Freedom Train', pointing the route north for escaping slaves. However, indoors the form of the original sign is shown, which was the regulation six stars in a circle and a seventh in the middle.

LEDBURY

The market town of Ledbury in Herefordshire has an above average number of timber framed buildings at its centre, the product of its unique history. It was founded by the Bishop of Hereford around 1125 at a crossroads, neither of which was a major artery, and given a town charter by King Stephen in 1135. One of its earliest surviving buildings is the chapel and hall of St Katherine's Hospital, set up as a charity for 'wayfarers and the poor' by Hugh Foliot, Bishop of Hereford, in 1232 (a family from the Plymouth area that we will meet again). Unlike most towns during the Middle Ages there was no effective local government because control was retained by the church. This continued until 1558 when the manorial rights of the bishop were confiscated by the Crown. Several local families then filled the power vacuum and promoted the clothing trade to their personal advantage by building fulling mills around the town. Wool from Herefordshire was highly prized and they could capitalise on exporting finished goods to the nearby trading centres of Worcester and Stroud where local regulations were more restrictive. The result was a dramatic increase in prosperity at the end of the sixteenth century.

The Seven Stars, Ledbury

For the first half of the sixteenth century, Ledbury was considered to be a very poor area with little or no new house building from 1500 onwards. Then between 1580 and 1610 as the new regime flourished there was a housing boom which produced many of the old buildings that can be seen there today. These have been described as being in the 'Ledbury Style' with close set vertical studding in between the main frames and a horizontal mid–rail, plus more refined distinctions.[13] However, this success did not continue. The population probably peaked around 1610 and a slump followed which lasted until the nineteenth century. The English cloth industry declined as a result of misguided protectionist legislation which damaged exports. This was followed by the Civil War when Ledbury briefly found itself on the front line between Royalist and Parliamentary forces. During the Georgian period Ledbury was too poor to replace buildings with the current style and people merely plastered over timber-framed frontages to give them a more modern appearance. Much of the centre of Ledbury therefore survived into an era when people started to value old buildings for their own sake.

The Seven Stars claims to be the oldest inn in Ledbury and has a plaque on it saying that it was built at the end of the sixteenth century. Comparison with other buildings of this period calls this into question and local research suggests that it first became a hostelry in 1526. It is on a street called the Homend, originally in the less select northern part of the old town, and it used to be opposite the cattle and pig market before the latter was closed in 1887. There is a surviving photo of a street party in the Homend to celebrate Queen Victoria's Diamond Jubilee in 1897 which shows the Seven Stars at that time. The front is plastered over with none of the framing visible.

In the early hours of the 22nd July 2001 the building caught fire. At the time the landlady claimed to have deliberately set fire to it but she was acquitted of arson in the following year. The building was gutted but the façade, the chimneys and many of the internal timbers survived almost intact. The old wattle and daub construction was cited by the fire brigade as a factor in its rapid demise and if it had been a windier night, large parts of the rest of Ledbury might have gone the same way. There was a threat to demolish it completely but its local importance was recognised and a restoration undertaken. It reopened in October 2003. The original timber framing is still visible on part of the front and in the bar. The interior has been modernised and some new additions, such as the window frames, tend to stand out as anachronistic. The main wooden framing of the walls is in an irregular and open style which strongly suggests that it is medieval rather than from the later period. It is distinctly different from the late Tudor inns in Ledbury such as the Feathers and the Talbot. A lot of dendrochronological dating has been applied to the more flamboyant buildings in the town but the Seven Stars does not seem to have rated such attention.

The Feathers,
Ledbury

The Talbot,
Ledbury

A brief association with Elizabeth Barrett Browning led to a Victorian library and institute being named after her but Ledbury's main claim to literary fame is that it was the birthplace of the poet laureate John Masefield. He published a lengthy poem called *The Everlasting Mercy* in 1911 which takes place in and around the town. It is a story of skullduggery, poaching, fisticuffs, hard drinking and wenching, which had a mixed reception when it came out, although the chief character, Saul Kane, is eventually saved by religion. In it the Homend is mentioned as well as a pub called The Lion which Masefield said was 'an imaginary tavern directly north of the Market House'. Many have chosen to see this as referring to the Seven Stars, although the connection is not exactly flattering:

> From three long hours of gin and smokes,
> And two girls' breath and fifteen blokes',
> A warmish night, and windows shut,
> The room stank like a fox's gut.
> The heat and smell and drinking deep
> Began to stun the gang to sleep.
> Some fell downstairs to sleep on the mat,
> Some snored it sodden where they sat.
> Dick Twot had lost a tooth and wept,
> But all the drunken others slept.
> Jane slept beside me in the chair,
> And I got up; I wanted air.
> I opened window wide and leaned
> Out of that pigstye of the fiend
> And felt a cool wind go like grace
> About the sleeping market-place.

After the restoration of the Seven Stars there was a suggestion that the name should be changed because the old one was unlucky. This idea was later abandoned.

There was another old Seven Stars to the north of Ledbury at Stifford's Bridge in the parish of Cradley. This was said to be 300 years old and the house next door is a listed eighteenth century building. In 2001 the landlady decided she wanted to call it the Prancing Pony after the inn in Tolkien's *Lord of the Rings*. Such is fashion (or perhaps even superstition). The building is still there but is now private housing. In the planning application the house was described as being eighteenth century.

*The Seven Stars,
Clehonger*

*The Seven Stars,
Hay-on-Wye*

Another eighteenth century building in Herefordshire is the Seven Stars in Clehonger, just outside Hereford. This is now a bed and breakfast, as is the Seven Stars in Hay-on-Wye. The Hay-on-Wye building is said to be from the sixteenth century and has the surviving oak beams inside to prove it. The town of Hay-on-Wye was founded around a castle built by the Normans in the twelfth century as part of the frontier with Wales. Technically it is now in Powys but its position on the eastern side of Offa's Dyke suggests that its main allegiance has always been with Herefordshire. In the 1970s it was declared to be an independent kingdom by one of the more influential residents and bookshop owners, Richard Booth, with himself as monarch. When he retired in 2005 the local MP said: 'His legacy will be that Hay changed from a small market town into a mecca for second-hand book lovers and this transformed the local economy'. It probably also helped the Seven Stars to survive, although not as a pub.

DAWES GREEN

Dawes Green is a small village in Surrey. Roman coins have been found there. Due to local reserves of ore and plentiful trees for charcoal, the whole Weald area from Kent to West Sussex was the centre of the main English iron smelting industry from the late Iron Age up until the seventeenth century, something that would be an anathema to many of its present inhabitants. Pre-Roman iron smelting remains have been found just to the south of Dawes Green near Crawley. During the reign of Elizabeth I the neighbouring village of Leigh was exempted from restrictions on the making of certain types of charcoal when cannons were required by the Navy. The industry had disappeared by the eighteenth century as emphasis shifted to coal fields in Northern England and Scotland to supply the fuel for smelting.

The playwright and first Poet Laureate Ben Jonson is supposed to have lived nearby at Old Swaynes Farm in Leigh. Dating of timbers at the farm has produced a construction date of 1470 and there are records of the family that owned it going back to the thirteenth century.

The main claim to fame of the Seven Stars in Dawes Green from our perspective is that it has a carefully preserved graffito on the wall of the original part of the pub which says:

> Gentlemen, you are welcome to sit at your ease,
> pay what you call for and drink what you please,
> William Eades, 1637.

The building must therefore have predated this as an inn or tavern. The management has a notice in the bar that Ben Jonson himself (who died in the same year) and even Shakespeare may have drunk there but there is no direct evidence for this:

BEN JONSON 1572-1637 ONCE LIVED AT SWAINS FARM

The Seven Stars, Dawes Green

A close friend of Will Shakespeare both being famed for drinking bouts in various taverns, Jonson was a tall gregarious, bibulous man, a soldier, dramatist and wit, who became the first Poet Laureate and received from the King £100 per annum together with a tierce of sack (42 gallons of spiced Spanish wine), Jonson visited Shakespeare's houses and there is every reason to suppose the "Immortal Bard" made trips out of London to Jonson's abode at Swain's Farm which is only one mile from the "Seven Stars" which was certainly in existence at the time.

The graffito on the wall of the Seven Stars, Dawes Green

Unfortunately, neither Jonson nor Shakespeare chose to scribble anything immortal on the wall, but then, if they had done, somebody would probably have stolen it a long time ago.

There are several other Seven Stars in Surrey. The Seven Stars in Ripley was an eighteenth century coaching inn on the London to Portsmouth road. It may have originally been known as Punters with a name change by 1801. It was rebuilt in 1927 and modernised in 1977.[14] A Seven Stars on Swan Lane in Guildford may originally have been part of the stables of the Swan Inn. It lives on in memory as one of the pubs that was blown up by the IRA in 1974, together with the Horse and Groom. Five people died in the latter but the Seven Stars was targeted later and had been evacuated in time, although several people were injured. The bombings were blamed on a group of Irishmen, the Guildford Four, who were convicted and imprisoned. These convictions were subsequently quashed and they were released fifteen years later. The building is now a shop.

The Seven Stars in Farnham dates back to the seventeenth century but was rebuilt in a pseudo-Tudor brick style in 1929. It closed in 2011 and is now a cycle shop. Farnham, together with Guildford, is on what is now known as the Pilgrim's Way, the route supposedly taken by pilgrims on their journey from Winchester to Canterbury. Some doubt has been expressed as to how many pilgrims used this track, as there is no mention of such a name before the eighteenth century. However, this was an ancient ridgeway route across the North Downs which probably dates back to the Neolithic era and may have connected to the ritual centres around Stonehenge and Salisbury Plain.

*The Seven Stars,
Ripley*

*The building
that used to be
the Seven Stars,
Farnham*

ROBERTSBRIDGE

Robertsbridge is a Sussex town on the London–Hastings road. Its neighbour, Salehurst, appears in Domesday Book but Robertsbridge was founded in 1176 around a Cistercian Abbey run by an abbot called Robert who built a bridge over the River Rother, the *Pons Roberti*, although this first appears in the record on Abbey seals from the thirteenth century. Some enthusiastic owners have dated the Seven Stars to this period but the present building started out life in the style of a timber framed Wealden Hall dating to the last part of the fourteenth century (for the technically minded this is characterised by curved timber brackets supporting the eaves, oversails on brackets supporting the first floor and a Crown-post holding up the roof). It was modified in later years and some have suggested that it was a private house up until the early eighteenth century. The nearby George Hotel was built on part of the Abbey's remains.

The Seven Stars, Robertsbridge

Robertsbridge was a prosperous market town by the thirteenth century, so it is likely that there were a number of inns there at an early date. Having been bypassed by modern roads, the village maintains a large proportion of early timber-framed buildings of which the Seven Stars is one of the earliest. Claims have been made by owners of the Seven Stars that there is a blocked-off tunnel under the building connecting it to the site of the old abbey which was about 500 yds to the north, and a curious, hidden 70 ft shaft is said to stretch from the loft and connect to the cellars, although the significance of this is left to the imagination. It was mentioned in 1576 as one of the most substantial buildings in the demesne of the local manor. The same enthusiasts also say that Charles II hid in the Seven Stars after the Battle of Worcester and a room was set aside to demonstrate this, but historically informed opinion is not convinced.

A view of the Seven Stars, Robertsbridge around 1910, from a photographic print postcard

Between 1734 and 1749 Robertsbridge was notable as the centre of operations for a bunch of smugglers known as the Hawkhurst Gang. The gang leader, John Amos, lived in the village and his confederates used the local inns for accommodation and fortification, on one occasion ambushing a wagonload of contraband tea nearby and killing a customs officer. In a letter to Richard Bentley, dated 5 August 1752, the writer Horace Walpole described part of his travels in the wilds of Sussex and his encounters with the local combatants:

From Summer Hill we went to Lamberhurst to dine; near which, that is, at the distance of three miles, up and down impracticable hills, in a most retired vale, such as Pope describes in the last Dunciad,

'Where slumber abbots, purple as their vines,'

We found the ruins of Bayham Abbey, which the Barrets and Hardings bid us visit. There are small but pretty remains, and a neat little Gothic house built near them by their nephew Pratt. They have found a tomb of an abbot, with a crosier, at length on the stone.

Here our woes increase. The roads row bad beyond all badness, the night dark beyond all darkness, our guide frightened beyond all frightfulness. However, without being at all killed, we got UP, or down, — I forget which, it was so dark, — a famous precipice called Silver Hill, and about ten at night arrived at a wretched village called Rotherbridge. We had still six miles hither, but determined to stop, as it would be a pity to break our necks before we had seen all we intended. But alas! There was only one bed to be had: all the rest were inhabited by smugglers, whom the people of the house called mountebanks; and with one of whom the lady of the den told Mr. Chute he might lie. We did not at all take to this society, but, armed with links and lanthems, set out again upon this impracticable journey. At two o'clock in the morning we got hither to a still worse inn, and that crammed with excise officers, one of whom had just shot a smuggler. However, as we were neutral powers, we have passed safely through both armies hitherto, and can give you a little farther history of our wandering through these mountains, where the young gentlemen are forced to drive their curricles with a pair of oxen.

Despite this involvement in the history of the Wild South-east, the main claim to fame of the Seven Stars in recent years has been its ghosts. It features in a list of the top ten most haunted pubs in Britain. According to that usually reliable source of alternative news, the *Fortean Times*, twelve successive licensees reported such phenomena over a thirty-two-year period. The correspondent suggests that some of these occurrences may have been encouraged by the stresses inherent in the licensed trade.

During the 1980s it was said that a noisy poltergeist cut holes in sheets, messed about with the connections on barrels and knocked things off shelves. Guests have reported being unable to open doors because of something pushing from 'the other side'. There were 'cold corners' in the rooms. The landlord in 2013 called in paranormal specialists to investigate such things as items moving, dishes skimming across loudspeakers, mattresses moving in the night, sightings of shadowy figures, footsteps in upstairs rooms, doors rattling during the night, televisions switching on and off, dogs looking at unseen figures and unexpected pokes in the back. The investigators recorded noises of doors rattling and eerie footsteps, and communicated with an entity who said he had been buried in a nearby churchyard in the 1600's. All this in addition to a Red Monk who is said to wander the rooms and appear in unexpected places. One landlord was sufficiently concerned that he moved his family out of the building. For those who are interested in such spooky relations and the paranormal, investigations continue.

BRIGHTON

Old Brighton and the Lanes

Brighton was known first in the Saxon period as Beorthelm's Tun and reappears in the Domesday Book as Bristelmestune. Up until quite recently it was Brighthelmstone, a fishing village on the Sussex coast that was one of the two main centres for the herring industry in England. When the fashion for seawater cures came in it became a place to visit for holidays, a fate that was sealed by the Prince Regent, later George IV, replacing an area for drying fishing nets with an exotic Indian style pavilion around 1820.

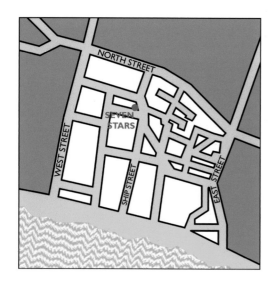

There is a painting in the British Museum showing Brighton being attacked by the French at the beginning of the sixteenth century. It was a small, square town bounded by three streets, imaginatively called East Street, North Street and West Street, and the shore line. The remains of this early plan are largely retained by an area of narrow streets now known as the Lanes. However, very little of the medieval town survives because it was all burnt down during the attack by the French, probably in 1514. Apart from being anti-English in principle, they seem to have objected to the smuggling and privateering activities of the inhabitants which affected their wine and brandy exports. The French tried to attack the town again in 1545 but by this time it had been rebuilt with brick and flint houses that were less inflammable and had a better warning system that allowed the assault to be repulsed.

The Seven Stars, Brighton

The Seven Stars in Brighton is on Ship Street in what would have been the middle of the old town. At various times people have claimed that it was first licensed in 1535, although the origins of this information are obscure and an inscription recording it on the front of the building that is said to have existed in the nineteenth century has since disappeared. The inn seems to have been there in 1692 and a deed exists with the name on it from 1785. The Seven Stars is also mentioned on a sketch map from 1778 in the East Sussex Record Office which records the locations of billeted soldiers.

The present building was designed in the best Victorian 'gin-palace' style by one Clayton Botham in 1897. Clayton Botham came from a theatrical background and also designed the Empire Theatre of Varieties in Brighton. The original design for the Seven Stars had even more minarets and griffins on it than those that survive. In recent years it has also been called the Helsinki Café Bar and O'Neil's Irish Pub or Flanagan's Bar, and has closed on a number of occasions. It has now reverted to its old name under more enlightened management.

FOOTS CRAY

Foots Cray is now in the London Borough of Bexley but for most of its history it was part of the County of Kent. The village developed on the main road from London to Maidstone next to a ford over the River Cray. Passage was improved by the building of a bridge during the Georgian era and the Seven Stars is next to this.

Between 2011 and 2013 the pub was threatened with being closed down and a vociferous campaign was launched in the local media to preserve it. This made much of the claim, based mainly on the opinion of a previous landlord, that it was 600 years old. It is a listed building and objections to a change of use stated that some of the structure, particularly the weatherboarding, may date back to the sixteenth century. Part of the original weatherboarded section is still there at right angles to the road but the main building parallel to the road was redeveloped between 1900 and 1910. A photo of Foots Cray High Street survives from 1900 showing the earlier state with weatherboarding across the whole of the front where the entrance is now. During the eighteenth century the Seven Stars is recorded as having been a coaching inn.

A noticeboard in the bar says that before the bridge was built the inn had a red light hanging outside next to the sign to warn people of the ford. It claims that the inn was originally a pilgrim's hostel and that an old sign (now lost) was found in a well nearby showing an image of the Virgin Mary with stars around her head. This issue of the Seven Stars and the Virgin Mary is something that we will return to at length.

The Seven Stars, Foots Cray

The same Seven Stars in a postcard from around 1900

KNOWL HILL

Another Seven Stars that has recently bitten the dust! Despite objections from CAMRA and others it was closed down in February 2012.

Knowl Hill is a village near Maidenhead in Berkshire on the old London-Bath road. In 1609 there are said to have been only five houses there. The first coach service to Bath was started in 1657 and took three days. The Seven Stars is known to have been a coaching inn. Its earlier history is unrecorded but it is clearly an old timber-framed building next to a coaching shed and barn of similar vintage. Press notices at the time of its closure therefore claimed that it was at least 400 years old.

The Seven Stars, Knowl Hill

While still a pub, it had its own skittle alley. It was associated with a nearby Star brick works. During the middle of the twentieth century it also acted as a local community centre and housed a doctor's surgery and a library. The present planning permissions

agree to its being turned into sets of luxury apartments, which may come as a shock to the four ghosts that are said to haunt the property. These are a horseman dressed in black, a headless woman, a phantom hound and another woman wearing a bonnet (and, presumably, still with a head).

The large image on the front of the building of seven stars without a name may have been the last survival of the original Seven Stars from before painted inns signs came into fashion (compare with the colour postcard of the Seven Stars on Withy Grove in Manchester). In this case they had been given an old French heraldic sunburst or spur form. Even these have now disappeared.

The wall sign at the Seven Stars, Knowl Hill

BOTTLESFORD

Bottlesford is a small village in the Vale of Pewsey, Wiltshire. The land has probably been farmed since the Iron Age and is known to have been inhabited by the Saxons. It is said to have been the main home of King Alfred the Great where he left his wife when he was off to war against the Danes. In return for looking after her, the locals were awarded an annual feast which is still celebrated in the Pewsey Carnival. In the Domesday Book Pewsey (or Pevesie) is recorded to have had forty-six villagers, twenty-four tenant farmers, six serfs and seven mills. Between 1450 and 1500 the land was owned by the Bishop of Salisbury. In a survey of 1737 the area had forty alehouses.

The Seven Stars in Bottlesford was first listed in directories in 1822 but claims its origins to have been in the sixteenth century. A postcard issued by the pub in the 1960s declares with confidence:

> The Seven Stars has been licensed for some 400 years. The inn was originally licensed by the Bishop of Salisbury as a brew-house and parts of the original brewing rooms still stand.

At that time it was only partly thatched. Any information about the pub's origins may

The Seven Stars, Bottlesford

still exist in early cathedral records. These are no longer in Salisbury but in the Wiltshire County Records Office in Chippenham.

There is another old Wiltshire Seven Stars in Winsley between Bath and Bradford-on-Avon. This is built of local stone and claims to have existed since the 1700's. In the past it probably had a thatched roof. The parish of Winsley was originally part of the manor of Bradford and from the time of Æthelred II to the dissolution of the monasteries was owned by the Abbey of Shaftsbury. On a number of occasions Winsley has been voted the Best Kept Large Village in Wiltshire.

Bradford-on-Avon was a well-established town in the seventeenth century. A survey of 1686 for billeting troops found that there were 102 beds available in inns there but, unfortunately, does not tell us the names of these or anything else about them. Bradford had a pub on the Newtown Road called the Seven Stars Inn which is now a private house. In 1722 the building belonged to a local clothier and is known to have been an inn by 1749. In 1793 it is recorded as containing its own malt-house and in 1824 a brewery was built at the back to supply the inn. Business must have been good because between 1859 and 1864 the owners bought the houses opposite, knocked them down and built an even larger Seven Stars Brewery for exporting their now popular XXXX beer. Later called the Newtown Brewery and then the Pickwick Brewery, this was bought by Usher's in 1920 and promptly demolished. By this time local residents were starting to complain about the steam and smoke produced by the brewing process.[15] Ushers sold the Seven Stars Inn in 1969 and it closed shortly afterwards.

The Seven Stars, Winsley

81

MARSH BALDON

Marsh Baldon in Oxfordshire has been described as a 'History Book Village'. Surrounding a 10 ha village green, it was founded by the Saxons immediately adjacent to the Roman road from Silchester to Alchester (roughly Basingstoke to Bicester in modern terms). The original owner was called Bealda, whose name transformed into Baldon. It is cited in the Domesday Book as Baldedone or Baldendone when its ownership was split between the Bishop of Lincoln and a chap called Miles Crispin. In more recent history much of the area (particularly the manor of Toot Baldon) was owned by Queen's College Oxford, whose residents used it as a bolt-hole during periods of plague and civil war.

The Seven Stars, Marsh Baldon

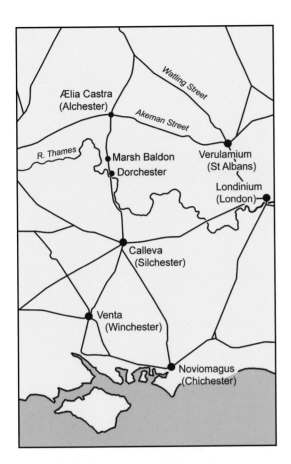

The distant history of the Seven Stars is obscure but it served a time as a coaching inn on the Oxford–Reading road. Recent publicity claims that it is between 350 and 400 years old but it has clearly been expanded in an ad hoc way over time. It was probably a well-served inn in the sixteenth and seventeenth centuries but, like many such places, it was deserted by its road and became somewhat of a backwater. While this relative isolation may have contributed to the survival of the village, it created problems for the commercial success of the pub. It has closed down a number of times in the past decade before being bought by a local business man. He then sold it to the newly formed Baldon and Nuneham Community Society Ltd run by local residents as shareholders. They appointed a manger and the refurbished pub opened in March 2013. A new dining area was developed from an attached barn which has a roof containing extremely ancient and irregular beams partly consumed by wood-boring beetles. The modern sign is a picture of The Plough asterism.

Above left: Part of the Roman Road system in the south of England

Above right: The sign of the Seven Stars, Marsh Baldon

83

SOUTH TAWTON

South Tawton is a village in Devon at the northern edge of Dartmoor. It appears in the Domesday Book as Suthawthune but its earlier Saxon name was Tauetona. At the beginning of the eleventh century the local manor including South Tawton was the property of Gytha, the mother of Harold II of Hastings fame. After the Norman Conquest it was owned first by William and was then passed to Henry I. South Tawton was on the northern circular route around Dartmoor next to the old Exeter–Okehampton road and there were other inns in the area, such as the Oxenham Arms in South Zeal which is said to be 800 years old and originally part of a monastery. The present building is regarded as being from the sixteenth century. The first record of local tin mining is from 1156. In 1377 there was a peasant's revolt in South Tawton against low wages and the privileged stannary laws of the local tin miners.

The Seven Stars, South Tawton

Early promotional literature for the Seven Stars in South Tawton says that it dates to 1603. However, whatever was there burnt down in the 1890's and the present building was opened in 1895. Built out of local stone, the ceilings incorporated old oak beams taken from nearby Oxenham Manor. It appears in local directories as an inn up until 1883 but from 1893 it was called a public house.

The appearance of the original Seven Stars may be shown by the old Church House which is immediately opposite. This was built between 1480 and 1520 and is regarded as one of the best surviving examples of its type. One of its main annual functions was to brew and house Church Ales. A complete set of Ale-Warden's accounts survive from 1524 to 1571, having been kept with the parish records in the nearby church of St Andrew. There were two Ale-Wardens at any one time and they were referred to as the 'Wardens of the Hoggenre Store'.[16] In later records the terms *cervisia* and ale were first replaced with the word beer in 1649. After Church Ales were outlawed, the building became a poor house but has since reverted to its parish social function.

The sign of the Seven Stars, South Tawton

The Church House, South Tawton

DINTON

Dinton is a village in Buckinghamshire on the old road between Aylesbury and Thame. Its origins are Anglo-Saxon (originally Dunna's Estate) and it is mentioned in the Domesday Book as Danitone. Its only historical claim to fame is that it was a sanctuary for the person who is believed to have executed Charles I.

The Seven Stars in Dinton is a sixteenth century building. It has been an inn since at least 1640 and is on a road called Stars Lane. It was recorded as the Seven Stars in lists of Buckinghamshire licensed victuallers in 1753, 1792 and 1827. Having been latterly owned by several large breweries whose tenants failed to make a business of it, it was threatened with closure in 2011. To prevent such a fate the pub was bought by a five villagers and is now owned by a consortium of sixty-six local investors.

The Seven Stars, Dinton

The inside of the Seven Stars, Dinton, with a slightly ominous Elizabethan message

STROUD

Stroud is a parish near Petersfield in Hampshire on the line of the old eastern South Downs route out of Winchester. There was a large villa there in Roman times but in the early Middle Ages much of the area was common ground between several manor farms.

The Seven Stars in Stroud is known to have been an inn in 1744, when it was bought by Charles Child. A later Charles Child sold it in 1818 to C.J. Hector for £350 'in the presence of the homage'. This is a reference to the procedure for conveying copyhold property at the manorial court, in this case from East Meon. The homage was the body of principal tenants. In 1844 it was leased by the brewers G. and R. Henty. On a map of 1840 it was one of the few buildings in the area together with a few farms and their cottages. In the late nineteenth century it was part of the Bonham-Carter estates, from which it was bought by Hentys. Later it passed to Friary and the Ind Coop. The present building is mainly a late Georgian replacement, probably about 1825, when the direct Winchester road was turnpiked. It now belongs to one of the few remaining old independent family brewers in southern England.

The Seven Stars,
Stroud

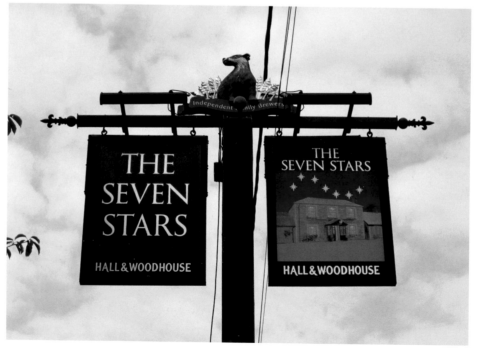

CANTERBURY

As the original focal point of English Christianity with the shrines of St Augustine and St Dunstan, Canterbury was one of the main pilgrimage sites in the country even before Thomas à Becket got his chips there in 1170. Some of the inns in the city may have started out as monastic hospices but there was a large commercial trade to be exploited once the pilgrimage business really got going in the thirteenth century. Pilgrimages created a great deal of wealth for the church and local businesses which brought condemnation from religious reformers such as the followers of John Wycliffe, the Lollards, who suspected the inns of supplying more than just a bed for the night. Extra drinking and sex were not what pilgrimages were supposed to be about, even if there were rules for when such things could be indulged in.

Chaucer's pilgrims famously left from the Tabard in Southwark but he does not mention what they did when they arrived in Canterbury. A less well-known anonymous fifteenth century addition to the *Canterbury Tales*, the *Tale of Beryn*, takes up the story.

> When all this fresh fellowship were come to Canterbury,
> As ye have heard before, with tales glad and merry,
> Some of subtle sentences of virtue and of lore,
> And others of mirth for those that have no store
> Of wisdom, nor of holiness, nor of chivalry,
> Neither of virtuousness, but of folly
> Lewd wit and lusts all, to such japes
> As troops of Harlequins caper in every hedge
> Through unstable minds, just as the green leaves
> Stand against the weather, just like them I mean.
> But no more here and now at this same time,
> In saving of my sentences, my prologue, and my rhyme.
>   They took their inn and lodged them at midmorning, I trow,
> At Cheker of the Hope, that many a man doth know.

Having set up at the Chequers as it was later known, one of the company, the Pardoner, takes a fancy to a barmaid called Kit who intimates that since her husband has recently died there may be more available than just bed and breakfast.

> The Pardoner beheld the rush, how people were being treated,
> Ignored it himself and stepped aside.

The Seven Stars,
Canterbury

(The landlord was being called all the time from one place to another.)
He took his staff to the barmaid: 'Welcome, my own brother,'
Said she with a friendly look, all ready for a kiss.
And he, as a man used to such kindness,
Grabbed her by the middle and made good cheer,
As if he had known her for more than a year.
She led him into the taproom where her bed was made,
'Lo, here I lie,' said she, 'by myself at night all naked.'

However, as is the way of these things, once Kit has spent the Pardoner's money on a slap-up meal, she refuses to let him in and he ends up sleeping with the dog after having been beaten up by her boyfriend.

We are told that the Chequer of Hope was built by Christchurch Priory around 1392 to accommodate pilgrims. It had a large upstairs dormitory that could hold one hundred beds. It ceased to be an inn around 1825 and much of it was damaged by fire a few years later. If the Chequer of Hope was its real name it suggests a religious conversion of the more conventional one of the Chequers on the Hoop. Explanations for this kind of sign have been varied. One is that it indicated that board games were played there. Another is that the chequer pattern represents an abacus and that money lending was available. This would not have been allowed in a Christian institution. The name does not indicate a religious background. It suggests that the Priory may have taken over an earlier inn and expanded it.

The proliferation of inns and taverns was not always regarded as a good thing. During the reign of Edward VI an Act was drawn up: 'to avoyde the greate price and excesse of wynes' and to limit the number of such premises in all English cities. Only four taverns in Canterbury were allowed to serve wine at any one time. The Act set prices and gave Justices of the Peace the right to issue drink licences. While price control of wine in particular was repealed under Elizabeth I, the restrictions on licences continued. Between 1660 and 1685 licences in Canterbury were only granted to the Sun, the Chequers, the Red Lion, the Three Kings, the Saracen's Head, the White Hart and the Seven Stars. Of these, the Seven Stars is the main survivor. The White Hart is now known as the Falstaff, and the Sun remains mainly as a tea room.

The present Seven Stars on Orange Street is an Elizabethan building with some modifications. It has been claimed that it was originally part of the accommodation for the King's School, founded in 1541 by Henry VIII and Thomas Cranmer, but histories of the school do not mention this. The Kent County Archives have a copy of a licence from the Canterbury City records issued in 1680 to 'Katherine Gill at the sign of the Seven

The old walled City of Canterbury and some of its seventeenth century inns

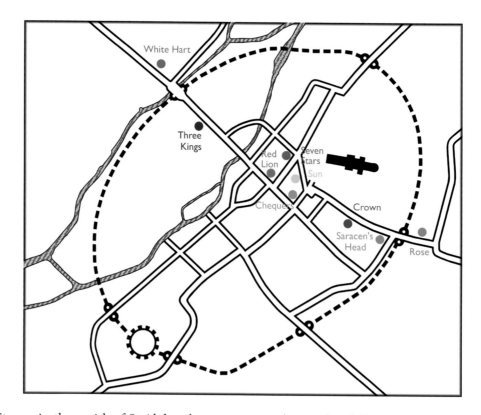

Starres in the parish of St Alphage' to operate as a 'taverne' and 'for wyneselling'.[17] This licence continued for a number of years whereas others inns lost theirs for disorderly conduct. In 1693 the Seven Stars appears in a list for billeting soldiers in which it was said to have room for eight. Over the next 200 years the name can be found in various notices for the holding of leet courts and in occasional adverts for letting, but in most of these it is referred to as the Fox and Seven Starrs.[18]

During the twentieth century a succession of earlier signs for this Seven Stars showed a hand appearing out of a cloud surrounded by seven stars. Ancient authorities, such as the Tory pamphleteer Tom Brown in his *Amusements Serious and Comical, Calculated for the Meridian of London of 1700*, regarded the sign of the Hand in a dubious light:

> And therefore I'll go back again into the Country of
> WHere being arriv'd I am in a Wood,
> there are so many of them I know not which to enter. Stay, let me see!
> Where the Sign is Painted with a Woman's Hand in't, tis a Bawdy-House.
> Where a Man's, it has another Qualification;
> but where it has a Star in the Sign, tis Calculated for every Leud purpose.

What 'every lewd purpose' was is left to the reader's imagination. Given this particular Seven Stars' location and good reputation such an interpretation seems unlikely. Canterbury town records contain a long run of police reports in which instances of prostitution and drunkenness were conveyed to the local magistrates but the Seven Stars doesn't appear in these. As well as serving as a court house in the eighteenth, from the beginning of the nineteenth century it was the Registered Office of the United Kentish Briton's Friendly Society. This was one of many parochial insurance companies which provided financial help in sickness and death for labouring men and their families in return for an annual payment. An image of the right hand of God appearing out of the clouds may be related to this and is very similar to, if not identical with, some of the symbols used by Freemasonry. The sign of the Hand-in-Hand was also used from an early time to show the presence of an insurance or a marriage office.

Above left:
The present sign of the Seven Stars, Canterbury

Above right:
An earlier sign for the Seven Stars, Canterbury

The Sun,
Canterbury

LONDON

The Seven Stars on Carey Street has the claim to being London's oldest surviving pub. This is mainly due to the previous sign which had 1602 written on it. Supporting evidence for this date seems to be lacking but the building is in the centre of one of London's main legal districts, between the Royal Courts of Justice and Lincoln's Inn Fields, where development started in the early thirteenth century as a result of a decree by Henry III that legal institutions should be outside the walls of the City. As a result of this sheltered location the Seven Stars avoided the Great Fire of London in 1666 which stopped a short distance away to the east near Chancery Lane.

The Seven Stars, Carey Street

The position of the Seven Stars, Carey Street, in relation to the Great Fire of London of 1666 (the extent of which is shown in yellow)

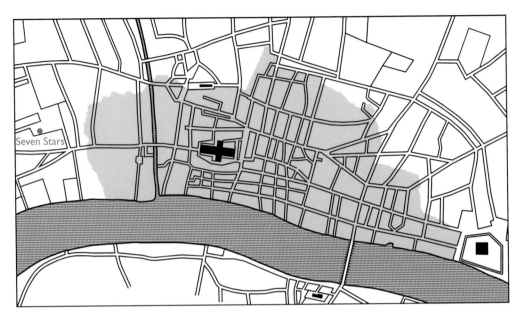

The old sign of the Seven Stars, Carey Street

It has also avoided modern planning developments in Fleet Street and Kingsway just to the south and west. It is in the parish of St Clement Danes which some have seen, without any actual evidence, as suggesting a Scandinavian connection resulting from Vikings settling on the north bank of the Thames.

Carey Street is named after Sir George Carey (1547-1603) who was a distant relative of Elizabeth I which ties in with the proposed foundation date for the Seven Stars. Nearby, in Portugal Street, there is The Old Curiosity Shop, only named after Dickens in the nineteenth century, but still a building said to date from 1567. The Seven Stars appears in various

parish records, trade journals and victuallers lists from the eighteenth and nineteenth centuries, and it seems that there was another tavern in the same street called the Leg and Seven Stars which some have claimed is a corruption of League and Seven Stars and relates to the Dutch Seven United Provinces which were brought together by the Treaty of Utrecht in 1579. This interpretation is as speculative as the one about the Danes. The present building has been modified and upgraded but it is suggested that the perilous stairs to the toilets are a reflection of its Elizabethan ancestry. One of the pub's modern claims to fame is the proprietrix, Roxy Beaujoulais, and her cat. This used to be black cat with a white ruff called Tom Paine. However, Tom has now passed on and has been replaced by Ray Brown.

Surviving trade tokens show that there were many other Seven Stars in London in the seventeenth century but most of these must have disappeared during the Great Fire. There is limited information on the ancestry of the few that remained in surrounding areas. The Seven Stars on Whitechapel High Street can be traced back to the Old Bailey's court records of 17 October 1744. Its publican, Edward Morgan, was on trial for being part of a gang that murdered one, James Sparkes, by bashing him over the head with a stave that had been taken from a local watchman.

Edward Morgan of St. Butolph, without Aldgate, London, was indicted, for that, he together with Michael Burchall, James Diamond, William

Harding, (not taken) with divers other persons to the Jurors unknown; not having God before their eyes, &c. On the 21ˢᵗ of August, in the 18ᵗʰ year of his Majesty's reign, upon James Sparkes in the peace, and God, and our said Lord the King then and there being; feloniously, willfully, and of their malice aforethought, did make an assault, and that he the said Michael Burchall, with a certain wooden stick, of a small value; which he the said Michael Burchall, then and there had and held in his right hand, upon the back part of the head of the said James Sparkes, did strike, giving to him the said James Sparkes, upon the back part of the head, one mortal wound of the breadth of one inch, and the depth of a quarter of an inch, of which mortal wound he languished, and languishing did live from the said 21ˢᵗ day of August, to the 7ᵗʰ day of September, on which said 7ᵗʰ of September, at the said parish of St. Mary, Whitechapel, of the said mortal wound the said James Sparkes did die.

Q. Who did you distinguish?

Howlett. Mr. Morgan.

Q. Did you know him?

Howlett. He kept the tap at the Bull-Inn, I have known him about three years.

Q. Do you consider what you say, this is a very material case, whether he did any thing, or whether he was only a looker on?

Howlett. When Parker, Sparkes and Appleby were knocked down, Morgan pursued me, and I jumped over Mr. Appleby, and Morgan was flourishing his stick at me, but being pretty nimble, I got out of the way, and I bid Appleby go into the watch-house, for he had got enough already. Then I saw Mr. Rawlinson, a Tallow-chandler, come to my assistance; one of the watchmen was going to knock him down; and I said, What are you going to do, don't meddle with him, I know him. Morgan was flourishing one of the watchmen's staves and said, You villains, what will you do, I will knock your brains out?

Q. How long was this after the watchmen were knocked down?

Howlett. About a quarter of an hour.

Q. How do you know it was Morgan?

Howlett. When Morgan was flourishing the staff, I asked Rawlinson, who that was, that was flourishing his staff, and he said it was Morgan, who keeps the Seven Stars in Whitechapel — Morgan said, You wicked vile Rascals, if you come up I'll knock your brains out.

Sparkes himself identified Morgan as the perpetrator:

> Eleanor Sparkes. I attended my husband in his last moments, and asked him if he knew any of the persons who had done him the injury, and he said the man at the Seven Stars [Morgan] and the man at Stepney [Harding] had done his business for him, and that he was a dead man.
>
> Mr. Harrison, Surgeon. I was present at the London-Infirmary at the time Sparkes [the deceased] was brought in: there was one Dadley and a third Watchman brought in as wounded in this skirmish; one of them had a broken skull. The Deceased had two wounds, one on the fore part of his head, a little above the ear; that was the wound his death was principally owing to: the other wound was on the back part of the head, but of no great consequence. — He was brought into the Infirmary the 22nd of August, and died the 6th of September of those wounds.

However, as a result of good character references, Morgan was acquitted:

> Mr. Ashley. Mr. Morgan is a well-disposed man, a man, that I believe would not swear an oath; he is the most peaceable man of any in the world; never any bore a better character. I deal with him.
>
> Mr. Fuller [the brewer]. I have known him personally about three quarters of a year, and he always, to my knowledge, behaved in a sober, regular manner, as an honest, quiet, industrious man, and bore an exceeding good character.

The Seven Stars in Whitechapel survived as a pub up until 2005 but was demolished in 2006.

There was a Seven Stars on Brick Lane which can be traced back to 1711 when it belonged to a Huguenot called French John. It was rebuilt in 1937 and closed down in 2002 after being a strip club for a while. It has been empty and undeveloped since. It may have been a meeting place for Oswald Mosley's British Union of Fascists in the 1930's. It also appeared in one episode of the TV series *Minder* in 1984. This Seven Stars' other claim to fame is an involvement with the screening of a short 'avant garde' film called *K Foundation Burn a Million Quid* in 1995. This showed two music entrepreneurs, Jimmy Cauty and Bill Drummond, burning a million pounds in £50 notes on an estate in Jura. The money was the profits from a pop group, The KLF. The film was originally going to be shown in a car park in Brick Lane at the back of the Seven Stars but at the last moment the screening was moved to the basement. Four hundred people turned up and the place was so crowded the film show was abandoned. The ashes produced by the burnt money were compressed and preserved in a brick which formed the subject of another film in 1997. People are still debating the purpose of these exercises. As is now the custom in this part of London, any free wall space is soon covered with examples of 'street art' of varying degrees of quality and the Seven Stars is no exception. In particular, the old car park round the back, Seven Stars Yard, has become the focus for this form of modern urban culture.

The remains of the Seven Stars, Brick Lane

100

Seven Stars Passage and Seven Stars Yard, Brick Lane

Another Seven Stars in Aldgate was associated with the notorious Whitechapel murders, some of which were attributed to Jack the Ripper. The victim in question was Frances Coles (aka Carroty Nell), a thirty-two-year old prostitute who was last seen outside her home next to the Seven Stars, Mint Place off Blue Anchor Yard. She was found by a patrolling Bobby with her throat cut in Swallow Gardens. A seaman, James Sadler, whom she had spent most of the previous day with, was accused of her murder but acquitted. She had not been otherwise assaulted and no money had been stolen from her. This vicious and apparently motiveless crime was the last in the series of the possible Ripper murders.

There was another Seven Stars in West Kensington which still exists as a building of some architectural quality. An inn on the same site can be dated back to 1799. It was rebuily in 1938 in an Art Deco style by John Nowell Parr who came from a family of pub architects. It was closed as a pub in 2010 and converted into student flats in 2013.

The Seven Stars, West Kensington

LEYLAND

You do not see a Seven Stars for miles and then all of a sudden two come along at once. This is what happens in Leyland in Lancashire. There is the Old Original Seven Stars at the beginning of Slater Lane, sporting a brick in its wall saying 1686, and almost immediately opposite at the corner of Fox Lane and Leyland Lane is another more prosaic Seven Stars. No public explanation has been provided for this combination. Near the other end of Fox Lane in the centre of Leyland proper there may once have been another Seven Stars which was merged with a pub called the Ship next door.

The Old Original Seven Stars, Leyland

Leyland first appears in the historical record in the Domesday Book and was sufficiently important to have had a hundred named after it, so it must have been there in the late Anglo-Saxon period. It was a relatively active area with two water-driven corn mills recorded near the site of the Seven Stars in the thirteenth century.[19] The Original Seven Stars is next to a crossroads which would have been outside the old town centre. It was marked by a medieval cross where the later Seven Stars is now. The main Roman road north from Chester to Cumbria, the *magna strata*, passed just to the east of Leyland. The Original Seven Stars first appears in as an inn in a census of 1871 when it was recorded as the last in the area to brew its own beer and had stabling for horses round the back.

The other Seven Stars, Leyland

There were several other Seven Stars in Lancashire but most have closed down in the recent past. One in Blackpool on Lytham Road was a coastguard station that was converted into an inn in 1856. It was later just called the Starr Inn and was demolished in 1932. The only survivor is the most northerly in the village of Stalmine on the Fylde peninsula north of Blackpool. The village is recorded in the Domesday Book as part of the manor of Preston and belonged to the de Stalmine family from the middle of the twelfth century. It may have had a prior existence as in recent years a Roman silver wine strainer and part of a Roman Road have been unearthed there. Local history suggests that the Seven Stars was built in the early 1700s.[20] The northern end of the inn next to St James Chapel was once used as a local mortuary and a Grey Lady is said to haunt the place.

The Seven Stars and its sign, Stalmine

105

DERBY

The Seven Stars on King Street in Derby is certainly an old pub, but how old, when it started serving drink and what it was originally called have all been matters of debate. It is outside the main part of the old city and is now somewhat isolated, having just managed to survive the nightmare modern planning and road system. When the original plans for an inner ring road were put forward in the 1970s there was a suggestion that the pub should be mounted on rollers and moved to a new site. This did not happen because of the costs involved but the Seven Stars is now on a traffic island and patrons have to brave the cars, trucks and buses on two carriageways of the main road and then step down below street level before they can get inside.

The Seven Stars, Derby

In the seventeenth century malting was one of the main occupations of the inhabitants of Derby. In 1693 the city had seventy-six malt houses and 120 alehouses. The brand name was sufficiently good that 'Darby Ale Houses' were springing up in London. For most of its history beer was brewed on the premises of the Seven Stars and only stopped in 1962. The sign on the building claims a date of around 1680. Its first mention as the Seven Stars was in the *Derby Mercury* of August 1775 when it was called 'The Seven Stars otherwise The Plough'. Before that it may have been a private house. It is about 350m from the western edge of the medieval St Mary's Bridge over the River Derwent and on the site of what was once the Augustinian monastery of St Helens. Up until 1935 there was a porcelain works nearby and customers were issued with china tankards instead of glasses. The oldest surviving pub in Derby is probably the Dolphin on Queen Street.

Ye Olde Dolphin, Derby

107

The Seven Stars, Riddings

Just to the north of Derby is the village of Riddings which has a Seven Stars built in 1702 on the site of a Chapel dedicated to St Mary Magdalene. The pub chooses to display a sign which only shows six stars and a notice giving a somewhat mixed explanation. On the one hand the seven stars are supposed to be the crown of the Virgin Mary, on the other they are the Pleiades with one star, Electra, missing following the standard Greek mythology. In a theory put forward by Graham Robb, Magdalene or Madeleine Chapels were originally Celtic religious sites. These were known to the Romans by their Gaulish name, *Mediolana*, and were positioned where the local Druids concluded that there were particular sets of solar coordinates based on the direction of the rising and setting sun at significant times in the year.[21]

KIDDERMINSTER

Kidderminster was originally a Saxon settlement which became the site of a monastery, Chedeminstre in the Domesday Book. With its favourable position on the River Stour for fulling-mills and transport, it was the centre of a medieval cloth industry. In Tudor times it was granted privileged legal status for cloth manufacture. When the business declined in the eighteenth century, it was replaced by carpet weaving. Starting as a cottage industry, this was progressively industrialised with the development of larger and more powerful looms, and Kidderminster came to dominate the nineteenth century carpet-making business.

There are those that claim the Seven Stars on Coventry Street is the oldest pub in Kidderminster.[22] To this end it has been ordained with the title Ye Olde Seven Stars. However, it seems to have been created by combining two private houses in 1792. The Three Tuns (formerly the King's Head) on the High Street probably dates back to the sixteenth century. There were other establishments such as the Courthouse Tavern in the fifteenth century. Ye Olde Seven Stars is supposed to have been connected to the River Stour by smuggler's tunnels, but its main claim to fame nowadays, apart from being a good pub, is that it is said to harbour a number of high-profile ghosts who have entered the record books of the paranormal. The main manifestation is of a White Lady appearing to be standing or sitting by the bar waiting to be served who, when looked at, gradually fades away. In our politically correct times it is perhaps best to say that this is a woman wearing a nineteenth century white dress or apron. Several customers and bar-staff claim to have seen the same thing over a period of one hundred years. She may be young or middle aged. Sometimes she has been called a Grey Lady. Other storylines suggest she was a girl who died on the first floor, or a previous landlady whose son died in an accident in the cellar where similar apparitions have been said to appear.

Ye Olde Seven Stars, Kidderminster

Elsewhere in the West Midlands there is a Seven Stars in Warwick which claims a date of 1585 for its origin. It is now a bed and breakfast hotel. A more modern Seven Stars can be found in Redditch.

The Seven Stars, Warwick

Below: The Seven Stars Redditch, and its sign

The Seven Stars, Ketley a month before it was demolished in 1964 (photograph courtesy of the Shropshire Star)

There used to be a Seven Stars in Ketley, on the outskirts of Wellington, which was reputed to have been built in 1579 and was said to be the oldest and best known inn on the road to Holyhead (originally part of the Roman Road of Watling Street). Records of landlords go back to 1740, and it was a main posting and coaching station on the road to North Wales. From 1927 it was owned by Wrekin Breweries but was demolished in 1964 and a new pub was put up, which was called Twenties and then the Elephant and Castle. This closed around 2000 and was replaced by an Indian Restaurant called the Blue Elephant. The old inn had its own mythology. It was claimed that the highwayman Dick Turpin used to stay there. Ghosts were plentiful, including a young woman, reputedly murdered, who walked around at night. A girl who was raised there said she used to hear mysterious piano playing from the bar downstairs at night. At the time of its demise it was in a very poor condition with uneven floors and iron truss rods through the upper rooms that held the wattle and daub walls together. For those with a morbid interest in such things, you can see a picture of the pub halfway through demolition in a photographic history of Telford.[23]

PLYMOUTH

The modern city of Plymouth expanded in the twentieth century and swallowed up many of its surrounding villages. One of these is Tamerton Foliot which became part of the suburbs in 1951. The name can be expanded to 'a town on the River Tamar that belongs to the Foliot family'. It was the richest manor in the area and is mentioned in the Domesday Book where it is said to belong to Alvred the Breton. However, at some early date after the Conquest it was owned by the Foliot family (variously spelt Folio or Foliott) whose most famous member was Gilbert Foliot, in turn Abbot of Gloucester, Bishop of Hereford and Bishop of London, before competing with Thomas à Becket to become Archbishop of Canterbury in 1161.

The Seven Stars, Tamerton Foliot

Plymouth itself was originally a fishing village that belonged to Plympton Priory. It was given a town charter in 1254. During the thirteenth century there were colleges of Dominican, Carmelite and Franciscan friars there. Under a law of 1390 pilgrims who were travelling abroad had to leave the country by either Dover or Plymouth. The port was a major importer of wine and hops during the fifteenth century.

Local history has it that the Seven Stars in Tamerton Foliot was originally a hostel for Plympton Priory during the fourteenth century, catering for preaching friars and pilgrims. It is near St Mary's Church, but nowadays has its own address, Seven Stars Lane. On the outside the building has been harled over but inside there are plentiful *The inside of* indications of antiquity, from low beams, odd shaped nooks and stairs, rough stone walls *the Seven Stars,* to the flagstone floors. The Plymouth Central Library has a photograph taken in 1966 *Tamerton Foliot* showing that the original sign was the regular circle of six stars plus one in the middle.[24]

The local geography of the Seven Stars, Tamerton Foliot

Kingsbridge to the east of Plymouth was a market town from the thirteenth century. The Seven Stars on Mill Street was opened in the 1840s by the Gibson family who ran it for several generations. In 1870 it advertised 'good beds, extensive stabling and lock-up coach houses'. At various times it also housed a dairy and the Kingsbridge Steam Fire Engine.[25]

The Seven Stars, Kingsbridge

CORNWALL

Until quite recently Cornwall was not well supplied with roads and the inns that accompanied them. Tracks and bridal paths served for inland communication. In the middle of the eighteenth century they were described as remaining 'as the Deluge had left them, and dangerous to travel over'. Pack horses and sledges served for carriers. Some towns even objected to the new-fangled turnpike roads when they were first introduced in 1759. However, what Cornwall did have was a lot of coastline and harbours (not to mention smugglers and wreckers). It also still has a disproportionately large number of Seven Stars.

The most notable of these is the Seven Stars on the Moor in Falmouth. As noted above, its antiquity is authenticated by the issue of a seventeenth century farthing token:

HENRY. PENIELL. AT. YE. SEVEN STARS. IN. FALMOUTH. 1666.

It is said to have been first licenced in 1660, having been before that a grain store in a building dating back to the fourteenth century. The present building dates to around 1800 and was extended in 1912. It has had the same family of landlords for the past five generations. The interior is determinately retro and is on CAMRA'S National Inventory of Historic Pub Interiors. It boasts a coffin hatch to the first floor (which you do not find in most pubs) and a world renowned, sixty-year old, collection of key rings in the bar.

Falmouth itself is a modern town, created around 1613 by a local landowner, Sir John Killigrew, on the recommendation of Sir Walter Raleigh who thought the place would make a good port. Before that there may have been a village there called *Peny-cwm-cuic* in Cornish (somewhat dubiously anglicised as Penny-come-quick). The headland just to the south had earlier been fortified by Henry VIII with Pendennis Castle to defend the Carrick Roads estuary. In 1688 Falmouth became the home of a monopoly for the Royal Mail packet station which dispatched all overseas letters and parcels to the rest of the world. This continued up until 1850, by which time Falmouth had been connected by a coach service to London and possessed a number of inns and taverns to service the resulting passing trade, particularly when they were kept in port by bad weather. In 1787 the gothic novelist William Beckford was stuck there while trying to get to Portugal:

> I thought last night our thin pasteboard habitation would have been blown into the sea. You cannot wonder at my becoming impatient after eleven days' captivity, nor at my wishing myself anywhere but where I am. I should almost prefer a quarantine party at the new elegant Lazaretto, off Marseilles,

to this smoky residence, at the mercy of the confounded keeper of the hotel, the worst and dearest in Christendom.

The Seven Stars, Falmouth

The poet Robert Southey described staying in a Falmouth inn in 1802:

> The perpetual stir and bustle in this inn is as surprising as it is wearisome. Doors opening and shutting, bells ringing, voices calling to the waiter from every quarter while he cries 'Coming' to one room, and hurries away to another. Everybody is in a hurry here; either they are going off in packets and are hastening their preparations to embark; or they have just arrived and are impatient to be on the road homeward.

The Seven Stars,
Penryn

Before Falmouth was founded, the original market town and harbour in the area was Penryn, which claims to be one of the oldest towns in Cornwall. It appears in the Domesday Book as Trelivel and was renamed Penryn by the Bishop of Exeter in 1216. The harbour was a main export route for tin and granite. In the sixteenth century most of the town's officials seemed to have supported their careers through piracy.

The Seven Stars is in Penryn on Market Street. A survey of eighteenth century housing in the town concluded that the present building predated that period and may be from the late seventeenth century.[26] A visitor in the 1970's was told by the then owner that it had been a licensed premises since 1454.[27] The writer was not sure about this but was prepared to accept that with the run-down nature of the property and the bulging walls it might be five centuries old. Postcards of the interior (which made it look like a yacht chandler's gift shop) that were issued in the 1960's quote the same date of 1454.

The Seven Stars, Helston

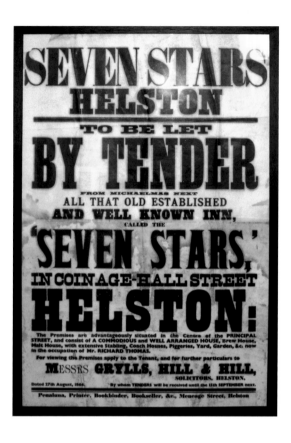

One of the main roads out of Penryn links it to Helston, the most southerly town on the English mainland, which has another old Seven Stars. Helston is mentioned in the Domesday Book as Henliston and probably predates that. Early on in its history it may have had a harbour until it became silted up. It was granted a charter by King John in 1201. In the Middle Ages it was a 'stannary town', which legally certified the purity of tin for export. It is best known now for its spring 'Furry' or 'Floral Dance' which has an ancient Celtic origin derived from the Cornish *feur* meaning festival. The Seven Stars in Helston is clearly fairly old but has little recorded history. The oldest pub in the town seems to be the Blue Anchor which may have been a fourteenth century monks' rest house that was converted into a tavern. Business has not been good. In 2009 the Seven Stars was offered free to any new owners, barring a charge for the fittings and fixtures.

Just to the east of Falmouth and Penryn, on the other side of the estuary, is the village of Flushing. Flushing was originally called Nankersey but the modern town was founded by the Trefusis family in 1661. Much of the marine infrastructure was built by Dutch engineers from Flushing in the Netherlands who gave it the present name. Most of the people who lived there in the eighteenth century were associated with the mail packets and it was a storage depot for the postal system up until 1850. The Seven Stars in Flushing is in a substantial building of Georgian aspect. There was originally another Seven Stars just to the north of Flushing in the village of St Just in Roseland. It was owned for one hundred years by members of the Tiddy family but no longer exists. The Seven Stars in the village of Stithians is just to the north of the road between Penryn and Helston. It was originally a farmhouse which was converted into a pub for the benefit of local tin miners in the nineteenth century.

A memorial to the postal packet service, Flushing

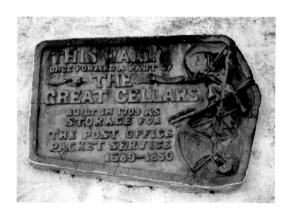

*Opposite, above:
A poster for the
letting of the
Seven Stars,
Helston printed in
1866 (photograph
used with the
permission of
Helston Museum)*

*Left: The Seven
Stars, Flushing*

*Below:
The Seven Stars,
Stithians and its
sign*

The Seven Stars Inn, St Austell

Finally, there is a Seven Stars Inn in St Austell, which has a well-documented history that goes back at least to the eighteenth century. It first appears in the records as belonging to a Mary Sawle in 1798. The Sawle family were Lords of the Manor of Tewington and could trace their history back to the Norman Conquest. The first named member that we know of was a John Sawle who lived in the town in the fifteenth century. The manor is mentioned in two different versions of Domesday Book as Bewintone and Deuuintona, later Towan. The Manor House still exists in St Austell, although it is now a dentist's. The family seat is first recorded as having moved to Penrice just to the south of the town in 1620. The Seven Stars was one of the main inns in St Austell at the beginning of the nineteenth century and brewed its own beer.

The Manor House, St Austell, built in a similar style to the Seven Stars

In 1863 the lease was bought by Walter Hicks, a local maltster and wine and spirit dealer. Apparently inspired by this to become a brewer, he then bought the much larger London Inn on Market Street and turned it into a brewery. Keen to expand, he then built an even larger brewery on Tevarthian Road in 1893 which is now the St Austell Brewery, one of the few old independent family brewing companies left in England. In 1925 Walter Hicks and Co. bought the freehold of the Seven Stars from Admiral Sir Charles Graves-Sawle. The Mary mentioned above appears in Burke's Peerage as the daughter of Joseph Sawle of Penrice, one time MP for Tregony. She died unmarried in 1803 and the estate passed to her nearest relative, Sir Joseph-

Graves Graves-Sawle, Bart. This presumably included the inn which was sold in 1925 by one of his descendants. Having belonged to the local manor for such a long time the Seven Stars must have been of some importance in the local infrastructure around St Austell. It is likely that an inn with that name or sign had existed on the site for very much longer and could have been in the Sawle family's possession for hundreds of years previously.

East Hill,
St Austell, with
the Seven Stars

With the tin mining industry, this part of southern Cornwall had probably always been a busy and relatively wealthy area with contacts to the Mediterranean going back to Phoenician times. In their heydays, ports like Penryn and Flushing always had a high proportion of foreign merchants in their population. Because of the essential and esoteric nature of mining during the medieval period, tin miners in Devon and Cornwall formed what were virtually states in their own right, with their own privileges, laws and stannary courts. The establishment of the mail packet business reinforced southern Cornwall's connections with the rest of the world up until the middle of the nineteenth century. The concentration of Seven Stars Inns in this region can be interpreted as part of these old trading connections, and their survival to the present day to the subsequent lack of more recent development until the growth of the tourist industry in the late twentieth century.

The rear entrance to the Seven Stars

Overleaf: The inside of the Seven Stars, Penryn in its yachting heyday

THE IMMACULATE CONCEPTION

In many books and discussions about old pub names you will be told that the seven stars are a form of religious symbolism and that they represent the halo surrounding the head of the Virgin Mary. At the Seven Stars in Foots Cray we are told about a sculpture (now lost) that was supposed to show this very scene. Somehow the stars become separated from Mary herself and developed an independent life of their own. Why such a symbol should have been relevant for drinking establishments is never explained. Maybe some have believed that certain inns and taverns started life as monastic offshoots and that some form of pre-Reformation Catholic symbolism gave them a kind of respectability and immunity from the condemnations usually heaped upon common alehouses.

There are, indeed, other signs that clearly have a religious significance. Thus we see the Angel, the Salutation, the Trip to Jerusalem, the Lamb and Flag, the Pelican, the Bishop's Head and the Three Kings amongst many others. There are all sorts of signs involving crosses, although many of these probably had a heraldic origin and derived from a local landowner who gave permission for an inn or tavern to open on his or her property. During the Middle Ages senior members of the church were often landowners in their own right and may have encouraged this process. Pre-Reformation names such as the Pope's Head and the Cardinal's Hat have tended to disappear. The question of whether the Seven Stars is such a religious symbol raises two issues: should the Virgin Mary have any stars to begin with; and, if so, how many?

Mary does not feature prominently in the New Testament and very little is said of her and her history. She is not mentioned by name at all in the Gospel of St John and only once in St Mark. St Matthew starts with the genealogy of Joseph who's 'espoused' is suddenly found to be pregnant by the Holy Ghost. Matthew's main concern was to confirm a prediction of such an event which had been made by the Prophet Isaiah:

> Therefore the Lord himself will give you a sign;
> Behold, a virgin shall conceive, and bear a son,
> and shall call his name Emmanuel.

In the second chapter we hear about Mary in Bethlehem with the Three Wise Men but after that she pretty much disappears. A fuller account of the Annunciation is given in St Luke followed by the story of the inn in Bethlehem that had no room and the appearance of some shepherds instead of the Wise Men. There is little here to foreshadow the role that the Virgin Mary assumed in Catholic practice over the next two thousand years.

The cult of Mary as the Mother of God (*Theotokos*) started officially in Ephesus in 431 where torch light processions were held in honour of her name under the direction of Cyril of Alexandria. Some have seen this as the incorporation of the worship of pagan nature and mother goddesses into Christianity to keep the locals happy, just as Christmas replaced the celebration of the winter solstice and Easter of the spring equinox (both based on astronomical calculations rather than anything to do with doctrine or history). However, after the success of the Main Feature people wanted more of the Backstory, so probably sometime in the second century someone wrote a Greek text that is now known as the *Book of James,* which is about Mary's family and early life. This is neither Gospel nor Apocrypha (not claiming to have been part of the Old Testament) but is a folksy story with a start that is based directly on the family life of Abraham and Sarah in the Old Testament.

A rich Jew called Joachim went to the Temple to present gifts but was refused entry by the priests because he had fathered no children. Grieving, he went off into the wilderness to fast for forty days (and forty nights). Meanwhile, his wife Anne was lamenting at home that the Lord had shut up her womb. Praying, she went into the garden and sat under a laurel tree. Looking up, she saw a nest full of baby sparrows and this demonstration of the fertility of the rest of the world did not improve her state of mind. And then, behold, an angel of the Lord appeared to her and told her that God had heard her prayers and that she would produce a child who would be renowned throughout the world. Another angel appears to Joachim and tells him to get home because his wife has conceived and to bring lambs and calves with him to celebrate the happy day. They met at the city gate and embraced, and the next day Joachim goes up to the Temple to check that he has been forgiven.

Nine months later Anne bore a daughter and called her Mary. For her first year she was carried everywhere so that her feet never needed to touch the ground. By the time she was three years old she had been accepted by the priests and was allowed to dance on the altar in the Temple. By the time she was twelve years old the priests were starting to worry that she might start polluting the sanctuary of the Lord but an angel told them to collect together all the widowers in Judea (including one called Joseph) and make sure that each was carrying a staff. The high priest took the staffs and a dove appeared out of the one that belonged to Joseph and flew off to settle on his head. This was a sign that he had been selected by the Lord to take the Virgin into his household. At first he objected that it would make him a laughing stock because he was old and already had a family but the priests told him it was the Lord's will and if he refused the earth would open up and swallow him.

Joseph then left Mary in his house and went away. One day she was selected by the priests, together with seven other virgins, to weave a veil for the Temple. By lot she ended up with the purple one. While she was engaged in this an angel appeared to her and told her not to be frightened because she had found grace before the Lord and would conceive through His Word. Joseph returns and is upset to find that his wife is pregnant. The priests are even more indignant and subject them to various ordeals to test for sins but they come through all of them. As a result of Herod's machinations they leave for Bethlehem and Mary gives birth in a cave. A midwife and a woman called Salome are at the birth. The latter refuses to believe that anything miraculous is happening and her hand is withered when she touches the baby, but after begging for forgiveness and confessing belief her hand is restored.

Although regarded with suspicion by some early patriarchs, this account became popular during the Middle Ages and was included in Jacobus de Voragine's *The Golden Legend* (around 1290). This was a compendium of lives and stories of the saints which became a bestseller all over Europe. Unlike the Gospels, the *Book of James* provided plenty of material about Mary's early life for artists to get their teeth into. Images of the stories appeared in many paintings and Books of Hours. One of the earliest to use them was the artist Giotto in his frescos for the Arena Chapel in Padua (around 1310). In forty panels he showed the essential scenarios for the Christian story so that those who could not read knew exactly what was going on. The first twelve are based mainly on the *Book of James*: *The Expulsion of Joachim from the Temple*; *Joachim Retiring to the Wilderness*; *The Annunciation to Anne*; *The Sacrifice by Joachim*; *The Vision of Joachim*; *The Meeting at the Golden Gate*; *The Birth of the Virgin*; *The Presentation of the Virgin in the Temple*; *The Presentation of the Staffs*; *The Watching of the Staffs*; *The Betrothal of the Virgin*; and *The Virgin's Return Home*. In these, as in nearly all images going back to the mosaics and icons of the early Byzantine Church, holiness is shown by a golden halo. There are no stars in sight (except for several hundred in the vault of the ceiling).

In many early paintings the halo was literally gold, being composed of gold leaf applied to a panel, sometimes with paint or embossed patterns on top of it. The origins of the halo as a religious symbol are not straightforward. It first appears in Christian art in the mosaics that were designed for churches and mausoleums of the Byzantine Empire during the fifth and sixth centuries. The first image of the Virgin Mary with a golden halo is a fifth century mosaic in the Archiepiscopal Palace in Ravenna. There is a striking image of Jesus with a large golden halo and cross in the mosaic of The Good Shepherd in the Mausoleum of Galla Placida from the same period. However, this imagery is complicated by the fact that other mosaics from the sixth century in the church of San Vitale have images of the Emperor Justinian and the Empress Theodora, both of whom are shown with golden halos. This reflects the symbol's pagan origins.

Giotto's
Bethrothal
of the Virgin
*from the Arena
Chapel, Padua*

The first halos are found in Greek images of the sun god Helios from the fifth century BC. From there they were transferred to other luminous gods such as Apollo and eventually to some images of Roman Emperors. These halos tended to be an aura of radiating lines in a circle round the head, reflecting an emanation of power rather than anything to do with sanctity. It may be that the technical limitations of mosaics turned such halos into simple circles that were the norm until realism started to take over the visual arts a thousand years later. Such a halo is sometimes called a nimbus but this was more properly the cloud that hid a god or goddess when they chose to appear on earth.

One of the scenes illustrating the Apocalypse from a triptych painted in Hamburg around 1380

The Virgin Mary acquired many other symbolic attributes over the ages, particularly in the colour of her clothes, but the next phase in her headgear developed from the sixth century onwards. The conversion of the Christian church from oppressed minority to imperial power happened fairly quickly during the reign of Constantine but it took a while for the church hierarchy itself to take over the mantle of temporal control in addition to its spiritual role. The Pope was originally the Bishop of Rome and was concerned with pastoral matters. However, the Papacy became increasingly drawn into the political sphere and started to exert control at all levels of society. Gregory I (590-604) took over some of the day to day running of Rome. Stephen II (752-67) took over rights to a Papal State. By the twelfth century this had expanded to cover a large central block of the Italian peninsular. During the early Middle Ages secular rulers were considered to be subject to Papal authority. The Papacy itself took on some of the regalia and trappings of imperial power.

Mary as the Queen of Heaven in the Ghent Altarpiece by Jan van Eyck

By the seventh century stories of the purity of the Virgin in birth had been extended to her death. With no clear tomb or cult centre it was easy to claim that she had not been subject to death and corruption like ordinary mortals but was translated directly into heaven. This Assumption was celebrated as a feast from the ninth century onwards, although it had been based on earlier tales of the Dormition where she did not die but merely fell asleep. The symbolism of the power of the church on earth was transferred to the Virgin Mary who became the 'Queen of Heaven'. As was fitting for a queen, she was fitted out with the necessary possessions, in particular a golden or jewelled crown which replaced her halo. By the twelfth century images of her coronation had started to appear, particularly in France. As the power of the church declined in the later Middle Ages, secular rulers who commissioned paintings and chapels for the sake of their immortal souls saw this imagery as particularly suitable. Later, even bankers and merchants used the same route for salvation.

There are many paintings and sculptures from the gothic period showing the Virgin Mary sitting on a throne and wearing a crown. One that is most interesting from our point of view is the *Virgin in Majesty* from the Ghent Altarpiece by Jan van Eyck (1432). One of the panels shows Mary, dressed in a pearl-edged robe, sitting and reading a book. On her head is a crown of pearls and jewels with lilies and roses attached to it. Above her head are a set of stars. There are probably eleven of these but it is difficult to tell because some are obscured by the crown. They are arranged irregularly and are definitely not a halo. It is possible that they are van Eyck's version of the constellation of Virgo (it hardly needs saying that this constellation's name was invented by the Ancient Greeks long before the Virgin Mary was dreamt of). The back of the throne has an inscription which reads:

> She is more beautiful than the sun and the army of stars;
> > compared to the light she is superior.
> She is truly the reflection of eternal light and a spotless mirror of God.

This epitome of divine light is consciously set against the heavenly bodies in a comparison that is more pagan than Christian but the reference may also owe much to the Book of Revelation which features in some of the other quotations in the altarpiece. This is our next port of call.

The Revelation of St John the Divine (or The Apocalypse of John as it is sometimes known) is the last book of the New Testament. It is supposed to have been written by St John while he was on the island of Patmos. It is distinctly different from the rest of the New Testament in that it describes an apocalyptic vision of past and future events expressed in wildly symbolic and visionary language. Much of this is so obscure that it can be (and has been) interpreted by anybody in their own way. In Chapter 12 we are introduced to a woman who bears a child in heaven which many have seen as a form of the Nativity. She has a crown of twelve stars on her head and the moon beneath her feet. It is worth quoting most of this chapter to remind us how bizarre the imagery in it is:

And there appeared a great wonder in heaven, a woman clothed with the sun,
and the moon under her feet, and upon her head a crown of twelve stars:
And she being with child cried, travailing in birth, and pained to be delivered.
And there appeared another wonder in heaven; and behold a great red dragon,
having seven heads and ten horns, and seven crowns upon his heads.
And his tail drew the third part of the stars of heaven, and did cast them to the
earth: and the dragon stood before the woman which was ready to be
delivered, for to devour her child as soon as it was born.
And she brought forth a man child who was to rule all the nations with a rod of iron:
and her child was caught up unto God, and to his throne.
And the woman fled into the wilderness, where she hath a place prepared of God
that they should feed her there a thousand two hundred and threescore days.
And there was war in heaven: Michael and his angels fought against the dragon:
and the dragon fought and his angels.
And prevailed not: neither was their place found any more in heaven.
And the great dragon was cast out, that old serpent, called the Devil and Satan,
which deceiveth the whole world: he was cast out into the earth, and his
angels were cast out with him.
And when the dragon saw that he was cast unto the earth he persecuted the
woman which brought forth the man child.
And to the woman were given two wings of a great eagle, that she might fly into
the wilderness, unto her place, where she is nourished for a time, and times,
and half a time, from the face of the serpent.
And the serpent cast out of his mouth water as a flood after the woman, that he
might cause her to be carried away of the flood.
And the earth helped the woman, and the earth opened her mouth, and
swallowed up the flood which the dragon cast out of his mouth.
And the dragon was wroth with the woman, and went to make war with
remnant of her seed, which keep the commandments of God, and have the
testimony of Jesus.

Whatever this is about it does not sound much like a jolly Christmas in Bethlehem, even with a stable full of fleas! It does not get any better in the next chapter where even more weird animals appear and the nasty people of the earth are marked with the number of the beast: six hundred threescore and six. These two chapters alone have provided most of the material for an endless number of exploitative and sensational books and

The Woman
Clothed with
the Sun *after
Albrecht Dürer*

films about Satanism and serial murderers. No doubt the battle between good and evil is involved but at which period in history it is supposed to occur is unclear. It may be that it is more a cryptic condemnation of the contemporary Roman Empire that was faced by the early Christians. Numerologists have applied their minds to the number 666 and many have decided that it must refer to the Emperor Nero. However, Christian iconography was keen on beasts of all sorts and many could be intimately linked to the Antichrist in one way or another.

At various times this woman has been associated with a number of contexts and these passages are still part of the mass for the Assumption.[1] An image of this scene was included in an English monastic manuscript in the middle of the thirteenth century, probably in St Albans. A German image of the Apocalypse that is almost contemporary with Giotto shows the woman and the twelve stars but they are completely separate. A great many medieval goose feathers were worn down debating the pros and cons for identifying this woman as the Virgin Mary and it was many centuries before the pros started to win the argument. Dürer's *Woman Clothed with the Sun* of 1498, faced with the seven-headed dragon, looks very holy but there is little evidence to suggest that she is being depicted as the Virgin, although she has acquired some sort of halo of twelve stars.

Various ideas have been proposed about the meaning of the twelve stars. Literal interpreters have suggested that they are the twelve tribes of Israel, twelve apostles, the twelve months of the year or the twelve signs of the zodiac. In his best allegorical mode, St Bonaventure said they are the twelve joys of happiness achieved by the perfected soul.

In the modern Catholic Church four fundamental dogmas underlie beliefs in the Virgin Mary: her virginity; her divine motherhood; her Assumption directly into heaven; and her Immaculate Conception. Surprisingly, some of these have received their final official formulation quite recently despite having been argued about for hundreds of years. Apparently there are people in the Catholic Church who are still debating whether the Virgin's hymen remained intact during and after the birth of Christ. This is part of the well-publicised problem that the Christian church has always had with sexuality.

The earliest creation traditions of the Middle East were largely amoral. People had been created to be servants of the gods. Morality entered the picture with Zoroastrianism. Death and corruption in the material world were the products of an independent power of Evil. People had been created to help the Great God Ahura Mazda fight this Evil. Eventually everybody would be reborn into a perfect world when Evil had been defeated. It could be argued that the whole story of the nativity of Jesus and the Magi was retro-engineered to agree with astrological events and Jewish traditions about a Messiah. These, in turn, may have been based on Persian astrological beliefs from at least the seventh or eighth centuries BC about the cycles of the ages which will come to an end with a Universal Judgment and the appearance of a final saviour, the *Saoshyant* conceived by a virgin, who will supervise the perfect world originally ordained by Ahura Mazda.[2]

The Judaeo-Christian tradition of the Garden of Eden narrowed this story down to one of sexuality. Eve had eaten the forbidden fruit of knowledge and become aware of her body and its functions. This fall from grace weighed heavily on the early Church. According to St Augustine, we are 'born between faeces and urine'. Asceticism, borrowed from Greek tradition, was the prevailing philosophy. True believers went off to live as hermits or castrated themselves to avoid evil thoughts. The culture of monasticism led to independent groups of men and woman living in isolation to intercede with the Almighty on behalf of the mass of corrupt humanity. Heretics who chose other paths were brutally repressed.

The Virgin Mary was seen as the antidote to the fall of Eve. In the words of Marbod of Rennes (around 1120):

> after the Lord, thou art the hope of men whom the mind conscious of sin
> consumes – the mind which is foul through the contagion of Venus.

By being a totally pure vessel for the birth of the Redeemer she bypassed the problems of all that nasty biology and lust. The difficulty, however, was deciding at what point this purity started. The dogma of the virgin birth of Jesus was a fundamental article of faith and could not be doubted. That the conception of Mary in the womb of St Anne had been achieved through divine intervention became a popular idea among the faithful, as in the *Book of James*, without them bothering too much about the theological or biological details. Feasts celebrating the conception of Mary started in the Eastern Church in the seventh and were introduced into the West in the ninth century.

Not everybody agreed with this and by the twelfth century the arguments started to become heated. Some, particularly the Dominicans, reacted against the celebration of the concupiscence of Joachim and Anne, as it could not have been anything other than physical and was therefore basically a sin. Others, to begin with the Franciscans and later the Carmelites and the Jesuits, used allegorical interpretations of short passages of scripture going back to Genesis to claim that the birth of Mary and Jesus and the triumph of the Christian church had been predicted from the beginning as part of God's great plan from the Creation onwards. Therefore it was predetermined that Mary could not have been born as anything other than pure and her Conception was Immaculate. She had been conceived outside the stain of original sin and not just acquired sanctity in the womb as the Dominicans and other apologists claimed. This split in the Catholic Church carried on from the twelfth to the nineteenth century. The Immaculate Conception only

The Immaculate
Conception
*after Diego
Velázquez*

became fully established as dogma in a Bull of Pope Pius IX in 1854.

The doctrine of the Immaculate Conception migrated around Europe and had become particularly popular in Spain by the sixteenth century. Artists started painting pictures of the Virgin as a young girl in isolation but these required agreed symbols so that the faithful could be certain of what they were seeing. The Spanish painter Francisco Pacheco compiled an exhaustive catalogue of such symbols which was finally published posthumously in his *Art of Painting* of 1649. Influenced by the visions of a Portuguese mystic, Beatriz de Silva, and the teachings of Spanish Carmelites based on the writings of the Franciscan theologian St Bonaventure, our old friend Chapter 12 of the Revelation of St John the Divine had been reintroduced as an image of the Immaculate Virgin, defined by the twelve stars over her head. This can be seen in one of the first paintings produced by Pacheco's son-in-law Diego Velázquez in *The Immaculate Conception* of 1619. This was commissioned by the Shod Carmelites of Seville, together with a pendant piece of *St John the Evangelist on the Island of Patmos*. The *Immaculate Conception* shows the Virgin as a young girl standing on the moon and with twelve stars around her head. These are clearly countable. Velázquez subsequently hedged his bets by also painting a *Coronation of the Virgin* in 1644. Later artists followed this lead but chose to be more realistic in showing the halo in perspective. However, it is quite obvious that we are dealing with twelve stars and not seven.

The Madonna in Glory *by Carlo Dolci from 1670*

139

Some may find this an overlong analysis of a symbol found on a mere pub sign (although it could have been longer and, anyway, we have not finished yet). What it makes quite clear is that seven stars are not, and never have been, anything to do with the Virgin Mary. If the sign of the Seven Stars was connected with the Catholic Church in England it is not through the symbolism of the Virgin. While such stellar imagery has been accessible for the last two thousand years through interpretations of Revelation (and has been used in a variety of contexts) the number of stars is wrong and the final formulation of the symbolism in relation to the Immaculate Conception was not firmly laid out until the seventeenth century. It cannot, therefore, be connected with inns and taverns that may go back to the 1300s or earlier.

THE BOOK OF ENOCH

Excluding the twelve stars from our survey does not mean that we have heard the last of The Revelation of St John the Divine (or whatever you want to call it). This book contains enough obscure symbolism to have fully occupied people for the last 1,800 years. It is also one of the major literary sources for students of the Seven Stars.

St John the Divine, whilst on the Island of Patmos (at least, so we are told), one day heard 'a great voice, as of a trumpet'. Looking round to find out who was talking to him, he saw, standing in the middle of seven golden candlesticks, 'one like unto the Son of Man'.

Among various other wonderful attributes (such as snowy white hair and brass feet), this individual had 'in his right hand seven stars'. The description is both vague and precise but St John was sufficiently impressed to fall at the feet of this vision in certain knowledge that he had a direct line to the Almighty.

> And he had in his right hand seven stars: and out of his mouth went a sharp two-edged sword: and his countenance was as the sun shineth in his strength.

The vision assured him that it was he that 'liveth and was dead', that he held the keys to hell and death, and that St John should write down what he saw. In explanation the apparition said:

> The mystery of the seven stars which thou sawest in my right hand, and the seven golden candlesticks. The seven stars are the angels of the seven churches: and the seven candlesticks which thou sawest are the seven churches.

> Unto the church of Ephesus write: These things sayeth he that holdeth the seven stars in his right hand, who walketh in the midst of the seven candlesticks.

> And unto the angel of the church in Sardis write: These things sayeth he that hath the seven Spirits of God, and the seven stars: I know thy works, and thou hast a name that thou liveth and art dead.

The Seven Stars in St John's Vision of Christ and the Seven Candlesticks from Albrecht Dürer's woodcut illustrations in an Apocalypse of 1498

The seven churches are named but the nature of the seven angels is less certain. Later on we meet seven angels who carry seven golden vials. These contain the wrath of God, which is revealed as the seven last plagues – sores, death, water turning to blood, fires, darkness, drought, thunder, lightning and earthquakes – the usual agents of apocalyptic literature that are sent to afflict the ungodly. However, there are other golden vials which contain odours that are the prayers of the saints.

The number seven is one of the leitmotifs of Revelation. Apart from the churches, angels, stars, golden candlesticks, golden vials and last plagues, we have seven Spirits of God, lamps of fire, seals, trumpets, thunders, mountains, crowns, kings, and beasts with seven heads, horns and eyes. Altogether, the word 'seven' appears fifty-two times in the book, far outnumbering the next numbers, four, ten and twelve, which appear about twenty times, and two and three which appear on eleven occasions. The seven stars are mentioned five times in four verses.

All studies of symbolism regard seven as a serious number. Many lists have been compiled of groups of seven, ranging from the Seven Deadly Sins to the Seven Wonders of the World. Interesting as these lists are, they do not really explain anything. Seven is beloved by number jugglers and kabbalists. This is not new. The Mother Goose Problem (as I was going to St Ives, I met a man with seven wives; every wife had seven sacks, every sack had seven cats, every cat had seven kittens; how many were going to St Ives.) is exactly paralleled by an Egyptian exercise in the Rhind papyrus dating to BC 1650. In the original Hebrew version of the first chapter of Genesis not only is the world made in seven days but, according to a previous Chief Rabbi Dr. Jonathan Sacks, the word 'good' is used seven times, the first verse contains seven words, the second fourteen and so on. The account of the seventh day contains thirty-five words, God appears thirty-five times, Earth twenty-one times and the entire chapter is 469 (7 x 67) words long. The intention was to demonstrate the mathematical structure and design of the world in the mind of God. None of this, however, explains why the number seven itself was important unless you take the fundamentalist position that Yahweh chose it to be that way.

The logographic numbers that we use in Western Europe are often referred to as Arabic numerals, although they really came from India via the Islamic world. The word names for these numbers are mostly Indo-European in origin with the notable exception of 'seven'. This is can be compared with the Old Babylonian *sebet* and *sebe* (male and female) dating back at least to the beginning of the second millennium BC. The word seven therefore stands out as having come into our language from an Old Semitic source. This emphasises its ancient and distinct nature as well as its importance to the ancient world.

From the beginning of Genesis to the end of Revelation seven has been interpreted by many people as a symbol of completeness. God chose to make the world in six days. On the seventh he rested so everybody else has to as well. In his allegorical analysis of Genesis the first century Jewish philosopher Philo of Alexandria is effusive about the nature of the number. He doubts that anybody could adequately celebrate the properties of seven for they are beyond all words, and then goes on to use several thousand to do just that. Much of this is numerology based on Greek Pythagorean doctrine, but it is transferred to the Old Testament and the properties of seven are equated to God Himself. He also finds groups of seven throughout the natural world. In astronomy, apart from the seven spheres associated with the main heavenly bodies, he is particularly impressed by the idea that there are seven stars each in the Great Bear and the Pleiades. Their number is an expression of the purity of the heavens which God has seen fit to place there for the benefit of humanity, so that people can navigate and sow and reap their crops at the right times of year.

This emphasis on design and numerology persisted throughout early Christianity. We are indebted to Pope Gregory in the sixth century for recognition of the Seven Deadly Sins. By the time of St Bonaventure we also find the Seven Holy Virtues and the Seven Pillars of Wisdom (based on a quotation from Proverbs). Bonaventure also promoted seven blessings of Christianity, each of which was further divided into another seven: the Seven Sacraments, the Seven Exercises of Justice, the Seven Works of Mercy, the Seven Virtuous Habits, the Seven Gifts of the Holy Spirit, the Seven Beatitudes and the Seven Endowments. Unfortunately for the philosophers and saints of the last two millennia, however, this prominence of the number seven originally had nothing to do with Judaeo-Christian belief but was an inheritance from earlier pagan moon worship.

Common or garden time (as opposed to the modern time of physicists) is, and always has been, based on the periods of the sun and moon. Juggling these is inaccurate because the periodic movements of the heavenly bodies are not simple multiples of each other. As people have tried to make calendars more accurate, they have had to introduce odd hours, days and sometimes even months to stop the predefined seasons appearing at the wrong time of year. Tidy minded priests have never liked this and would have preferred that days, months and years were simply related to each other. To begin with they tried to make them so. Many such idealists were convinced that the year should consist of twelve lunar months of thirty days each even though it must have been obvious from early on that the solar year was nearer to 365 days. Some may have seen seven in a numerological and astral relationship as the triangular number $1+2+3+4+5+6+7 = 28$ which is an approximation to the sidereal lunar month – the time the moon takes to get back to the same position in relation to the stars. The synodic lunar month – what ordinary people see in the sky – is nearer to thirty days. True lunar months contain either twenty-nine or thirty days but in religious contexts people preferred to think in terms of idealised cycles.

Institutions that ritualised the seventh day of the lunar month are known from the earliest literature of the Middle East. There are Sumerian texts from the period of the Third Dynasty of Ur (around BC 2100) showing that special cultic offerings were made to the moon god (Suen or Nanna) on the days of the new moon, at the first quarter (the seventh day) and at the full moon. The Old Babylonian *Atrahasis* epic from around BC 1700 is the first description we have of the Flood. In it one of the three great gods, Enki, instructs the goddess Nintu to create human beings to do the god's labours for them. She does this by sacrificing another god and mixing his flesh and blood with clay. In order that he, himself, is fit for this work of creation, Enki swears to the other gods that he will have a purifying bath on the first, seventh and fifteenth of the month.

In the Babylonian creation epic *Enuma Elish* from around BC 1200 the supreme god of Babylon Marduk:

had Nannaru (the moon) appear and entrusted the night to him. He made him known as the jewel of the night in order to show the days. "Every month, without interruption, use your crown to shine above the land at the beginning of every month, illuminate the horns to show the six days. On the seventh the crown will be halved, on the 15th day it is in balance, in the middle of every month. When Shamash (the sun) looks at you from the base of heaven, as he agrees, decrease and grow backwards. On the day of disappearance (the New Moon) approach close to the path of Shamash so that on the 30th day you are in balance, be the double of Shamash".[1]

There is little doubt that seven was one of the most significant numbers in the ancient Middle East and was originally linked to the phases of the moon. *Shabattu* was one of the words used in Akkadian for the Full Moon and is generally considered to be the origin of the Hebrew Sabbath.[2]

Propitiation of the waxing and waning moon probably goes far back into prehistory, certainly to the Sumerians who predated the Old Semitic Babylonian and Assyrian cultures. The Seven Stars seems to have become involved in this as part of a catch-all symbolic scenario. Therefore the sign clearly had a religious significance in terms of the Revelation of St John and this was generally recognised, as can be seen in Albrecht Dürer's woodcut of 1498 for the first in his series of prints of the Apocalypse. However, the last book of the New Testament, while it may appear unique in that context, is part of a much larger corpus of apocalyptic literature going back to the earliest religious epics of the ancient Near East where the gods became irritated by the behaviour of humanity and sent floods and plagues to reduce their subject's numbers. The Seven Stars is involved here in another arena of symbolism.

There are a number of apocalyptic works from the first centuries BC and AD which were revered by some Jewish and early Christian sects in the Middle East but which were never accepted into the official canon of scripture. One of these is the Book of Enoch. Enoch was a Jewish patriarch who appears in Genesis. He was the seventh firstborn after Adam. His father was Jared. Jared fathered Enoch when he was 162 years old, and lived for 962 years in all. Enoch fathered Methuselah when he was he was 65 years old and lived for 365 years after which, being favoured by God like the Virgin Mary, he was translated directly to heaven. Methuselah held the record for longevity and survived for 969 years. He was the grandfather of Noah of Flood fame. These exaggerated life spans are similar to the ones seen in the early Sumerian and Babylonian King Lists from the second millennium BC and were probably produced in imitation of them. Enoch may have been modelled on King Enmenduranna, the seventh antediluvian king on the

Sumerian King List, who lived for 26,000 years and received special revelations from the sun god Shamash (interestingly Enoch was said to have lived for 365 years, matching the days of the solar calendar).

The First Book of Enoch (the Ethiopic Enoch) was originally written in Hebrew or Aramaic and later translated into Greek. It only survived in the Church in Ethiopia. The first translation into English was published in 1800. The Second Book of Enoch (the Slavonic Enoch) was a Hebrew work that was favoured by the Christian Church in Eastern Europe. It was first translated into English in 1896. Fragments in Aramaic of a Book of Enoch were also found among the Dead Sea Scrolls. All these books consist of an assortment of different texts dating to various times over the first century BC.

In this Apocalyptic literature, evil in the world was not primarily a product of the Garden of Eden but was the result of a gang of fallen angels coming down to earth and taking human wives during the time of Jared. They revealed the secrets of heaven to their offspring and taught them charms, knowledge of plants, flesh eating, bloodlust and the making of sacrilegious ornaments and weapons. Their spreading of unholiness, depravity and warfare everywhere meant that they were the ones who needed to be exterminated by the coming conflagration and flood. Godly people would survive and repopulate the earth, although they would no longer live for hundreds of years.

> And the high mountains will be shaken,
> And the high hills shall be made low,
> And shall melt like wax before the flame
>
> And the earth shall be wholly rent in sunder,
> And all that is upon the earth shall perish,
> And there shall be judgement upon all men.
>
> And with the righteous He will make peace,
> And will protect the elect,
> And mercy shall be upon them.
>
> And they shall all belong to God,
> And they shall be prospered,
> And they shall all be blessed.
>
> And he will help them all,
> And light shall appear to them,
> And he will make peace with them.

> And behold! He cometh with ten thousands of His holy ones,
> To execute judgement upon all,
> And to destroy all the ungodly.
>
> And to convict all flesh
> Of all the works of their ungodliness which they have ungodly committed,
> And of all the hard things that ungodly sinners have spoken against Him.

There is always an ambiguity in these apocalyptic stories in that they describe somebody from the past having a vision of the future. There have been people of all eras who have thought that the world around them needs to be cleansed. In the Old Testament the time sequence of Noah's Flood is straightforward and follows the Mesopotamian model but in the Book of Enoch Noah's story is often mixed up with an apocalypse of fire and earthquakes that has no clear time frame. At one point his Ark becomes a building that that is to be put up by the angels. Taken literally, the apocalypse story is of a small number of 'the chosen' or 'the elect' who feel themselves subject to the great powers of the day (Babylon, Rome, take your pick) and who fantasise that their God (of course, the only one) will bring them justice and a perfect or eternal life by destroying the rest of the human race in torment, firm in their own belief that this will involve them in no guilt for the ensuing holocaust. Such a message is still with us. Many of a Christian evangelical bent nowadays look forward to the Day of Judgement that is still to come.

While all this antediluvian mayhem was going on, Enoch, 'the scribe of righteousness', seems to have been hiding in a cave somewhere. He was called forth to intercede between God and the fallen angels. In a dream he is carried to the heavens and given a guided tour by the good archangels who run things up there on behalf of the Almighty. Finally, the Lord tells him that there is no hope for the fallen and, like St John, he sees the coming apocalypse.

> And I proceeded and saw a place which burns day and night, where there are seven mountains of magnificent stones, three towards the east, and three towards the south. And as for those towards the east one was of coloured stone, and one of pearl, and one of jacinth, and those towards the south of red stone. But the middle one reached to heaven like the throne of God, of alabaster, and the summit of the throne was of sapphire. And I saw a flaming fire. And beyond these mountains is a region, the end of the great earth: there the heavens were completed. And I saw a deep abyss, with columns of heavenly fire, and among them I saw columns of fire fall, which

were beyond measure alike towards the height and towards the depth. And beyond the abyss I saw a place which had no firmament of the heaven above, and no firmly founded earth beneath it: there was no water upon it, and no birds, but it was a waste and horrible place. And there I saw seven stars of heaven bound together in it, like great mountains and burning with fire. Then I said: "For what sin are they bound, and on what account have they been cast hither?" Then Uriel, one of the holy angels, who was with me, and was chief over them, said: "Enoch, why dost thou ask, and why art thou eager for the truth? This place is the end of heaven and earth: this has become a prison for the stars and the host of heaven. And the stars which roll over the fire are they which have transgressed the commandment of the Lord in the beginning of their rising, because they did not come forth at their appointed times. And He was wroth with them, and bound them till the time when their guilt should be consummated even for ten thousand years."

And from thence I went to another place, which was still more horrible than the former, and I saw a horrible thing: a great fire there which burnt and blazed, and the place was cleft as far as the abyss., being full of great descending columns of fire: neither its extent nor magnitude could I see, nor could I see, nor could I conjecture. Then I said: "How fearful is the place and how terrible to look upon!" Then Uriel answered me, one of the holy angels who was with me, and said unto me: "Enoch why hast thou such fear and affright?" And I answered: "Because of this fearful place, and because the spectacle of the pain." And he said unto me: "This place is the prison of the angels, and here they will be imprisoned for ever."[3]

Significant parts of the books of Enoch are concerned with astronomy but much of it is not the astronomy of an observational science as we know it from the Greeks or even the Babylonians. It is couched in much more mystical and symbolic terms. It was suggested by early translators that some of the books were produced by Jewish sects who promoted the Persian solar year to replace the Babylonian lunar calendar of 360 days so that holy festivals fell on the right days. Those who disagreed with them were subject to the apocalyptic hyperbole characteristic of Old Testament prophets. Therefore, when they speak of stars we must presume that they are referring to some form of celestial reality and are not just using a kind of allegory.

Revelations tells us that there are seven angels and older Jewish tradition highlights the seven archangels of Enoch – Uriel (leader of the heavenly hosts), Raphael, Raguel, Michael, Sariel, Gabriel and Remiel. The religious beliefs of the Yezidis (the least successful race of Chosen People) revolve almost solely around seven angels who run the world, God himself having retired and taken a back seat. The chief of these is the Peacock Angel *Shams-ed-din* (the Sun of the Faith) who, after having fallen through pride, repented his sins and was put in charge of the world. As a result the Yezidis are sometimes popularly described as Devil Worshippers. This tradition may have originated from much older Iranian beliefs based on astral mythology.

If we interpret angels as visible luminaries, it is tempting to equate fallen angels with the sightings of large meteors burning up in the atmosphere. One school of thought has gone as far as to suggest that within early human memory a large asteroid hit the earth and broke up in the atmosphere into seven pieces, thus bringing about the catastrophic events that were at the core of later apocalyptic ideas. However, until somebody finds some suitable craters, this has to remain a minority opinion. The seven stars in *I Enoch* seem to have been damned because they did not conform to the regularity of the rest of the cosmos but they are not the fallen angels. In one passage, twenty-one chiefs of these are named and they presided over hundreds of others. Another time there are said to be two hundred. It is possible that the seven are meant to be the sun, the moon and five major planets which were seen to move about the sky in a manner which is different from the background stars. In mediaeval Neoplatonic thought each of the seven spheres which constituted the cosmos was given an angel to guard over it.

The nature of these seven stars has to remain in doubt. Furthermore, the question we have to ask is whether any of these ideas could have influenced the people who named English inns and public houses during the past seven hundred years. Naming a pub after an apocalyptic symbol doesn't seem like a very good basis for trade unless people were just drowning their sorrows in the face of the impending doom. There are no pubs called the Four Horsemen of the Apocalypse or the Whore of Babylon. While the Book of Enoch was current at the time of Christ, unlike the Revelation of St John it was not part of Western medieval culture and only persisted in the Ethiopian and Eastern European Orthodox churches. Translations of these texts were not available in English before the start of the nineteenth century although some aspects of this tradition may have persisted in esoteric culture. The seven stars in Revelation, while still seeming to be angels, are a pale imitation of those in *I Enoch* and are marginal to our main story.

THE MASONS

In the original *History of Signboards* by Jacob Larwood and John Camden Hotten, published in 1866, the Seven Stars brand is included in the 'Miscellaneous' category and little is said about it other than this opaque statement:

> These SEVEN STARS have always been great favourites; they seem to be the same pleiad which is used as a Masonic emblem—a circle of six stars, with one in the centre; but to tell to ears profane, what this emblem means, would be disclosing the sacred arcana;

(or, in other words, we could tell you but then we would have to kill you!). For whatever reasons, this reference to sacred arcana was excluded from later editions.

Freemasonry claims to have its roots in the guild of people who built the first European cathedrals. They, in turn, it is said, could trace their craft back to the architect of the first Temple of Solomon in Jerusalem. These were 'Operative Freemasons' who actually designed and built things ranging from churches to sundials and who needed secret signs and words to check that other people were genuine members of the craft. However, by the seventeenth century a new brand of freemasonry had appeared, 'Speculative Freemasons', made up of groups of self-selected private individuals (albeit some of them in public positions) with a complex variety of ritual and symbolic activities that set them apart from the rest of society. Their actual link with ancient building trades can, to some extent, be demonstrated in Scotland but in England the connection is much more obscure. Speculative Freemasonry, a term first used in 1757, has been defined as:

> A peculiar system of morality veiled in allegory and illuminated by symbols.

Freemasonry has never claimed to be a religion but still insists in belief in a single God, although apart from any particular creed. During the nineteenth century the emphasis was strongly towards Protestantism but it may be that the ritual and secrecy originally came from some of the earliest lodges being formed from Jacobite cells in the seventeenth and eighteenth centuries when they genuinely needed to be secret societies. Bonnie Prince Charlie himself, who may have been a mason when he lived in Rome, signed a warrant in Derby in 1745 for the establishment of a lodge at Longnor in Staffordshire.[1] Others claim that the craft inherited survivors of the Knights Templar who went underground after persecution in the fourteenth century.

Opposite: Masonic symbols from the frontpiece to Jachin and Boaz, *published in London in 1776*

However this may be, by the seventeenth century modern Freemasonry had developed an origin myth, written down in the *Old Charges*, which was based on passages from the Bible, the apocalyptic literature and the Jewish histories of Flavius Josephus from the end of the first century AD. In this the sons of Lamech invented geometry but fearing the Wrath of God and the Great Fire and Flood to come, one of them, Jabal, wrote down this knowledge on two pillars of stone. One of the grandsons of Noah, Hermes, found one of them and the other was discovered by Pythagoras. They transmitted the knowledge to their descendants. The Babylonians and the Assyrians used it to build their temples and Abraham visited Egypt and taught it there. Abraham's clerk, Euclid, taught the Egyptians how to put up buildings of all kinds and founded the Craft of Architecture.

> And thus was the Craft governed there; and that worthy Clark Euclid gave it the name of Geometry; and now it is called through all this land Masonry.

King David brought such Masons from many lands to build a Temple in Jerusalem which was finished by his son Solomon. These Masons then dispersed across Europe and some of them were brought to England by St Alban.[2]

The original pillars developed lore of their own. In one story it was Eve who told Seth to record the words of the Archangel Michael on tablets of stone. In another, Jabal (or Jubal) made two pillars, one of brick and the other of marble, on which he recorded either the laws of astronomy or of music. Solomon's architect, Hiram, made two pillars of brass which were hollow in order to store the archives of Masonry. These were put up at the front of the Temple. One was called Boaz and the other Jachin. In another construction, Zoroaster inscribed all the knowledge of the liberal arts on fourteen columns, seven of brass and seven of brick to preserve them from destruction.[3]

Having fantasised that nearly every well-known intellectual from the ancient world must have been involved in their formation, Freemasons also absorbed many Apocalyptic and Hermetic symbols with an additional input from the Neoplatonic disciplines of astrology and alchemy where hidden and obscure meaning was a necessary part of communication among initiates. One of these adopted symbols was the Seven Stars which appears in many images of masonic paraphernalia, on masonic medals and is frequently used as lodge name. This could have come from a number of sources but the apocalyptic literature is the most likely. However, it was adapted by the Freemasons to their own purposes. At the public level this symbol now refers to the seven liberal arts (although there may be hidden meanings to which the public does not have access). These were enumerated by medieval scholars based on classical sources. They are the trivium of grammar, rhetoric and logic, and the quadrivium of geometry, arithmetic, music and astronomy. Freemasonry elevates Geometry to the first place.

Speculative Freemasonry started to develop during the Restoration period when scientific and philosophical societies of all kinds were being founded in British cities. Most of these met in inns and taverns, as these were the only public buildings available. In 1717 there were only four (or maybe six) Masonic lodges in London (possibly the whole of England). By 1735 there were 129 in England, one of which was called the Seven Stars (at the Royal Exchange in the City).

The first Grand Lodge meeting was held in 1717 in the Goose and Gridiron alehouse near St Paul's Churchyard. This may have had a political purpose to endorse the new Hanoverian rule and to purge masonic elements of old Jacobite sympathies. The other lodges present came from the Crown alehouse (Parkers Lane), the Apple Tree Tavern (Charles Street) and the Rummer and Grapes Tavern (Westminster). Shortly afterward there were lodges at the Cheshire Cheese (Arundel Street) and the Horn Tavern (Westminster). Inns and taverns recorded as housing masonic meetings during the first half of the eighteenth century were the Queen's Head (Hollis Street), the George (Long Acre), the King's Arms Tavern (St Paul's), the Devil (Temple Bar), the Crown and Anchor (Strand), the Three Compasses (London), the Swan (Chichester), the Carpenter's Arms (York) and the Nag's Head & Star (Carmarthen).[4]

In 1732 *The Universal Spectator* published an article about the Mayor of Canterbury attacking a meeting of local Freemasons:

> Whereas a Report runs through the Cyte, Town and Country, of an unlawful Assembly of a number of men that met together at a Tavern in this Cyte, and their bound themselves under wicked Obligations to do something, that may prove of sad Effect, therefore the Mare of this Cyte desires any Parson that can, to inform him aright, because the whole truth ought to be know, that such Dark-Lanthorns may be brought to light.

The tavern in question was the Red Lion, despite the fact that there was a Seven Stars available nearby in Orange Street which was sufficiently well regarded to hold leet courts in between 1737 and 1798.[5] As early as 1724 complaints were being made about excessive intemperance at some lodge meetings, with liquor undermining the 'Glorious Seat of Reason which the Divine Architect has honoured the Human Constitution.' One can also recall the scene from Harold Brighouse's play *Hobson's Choice*, set in Salford in the 1880's, where the three sisters are talking about their bootmaker father: 'Has he had breakfast yet, Maggie?' 'Breakfast! With a Masons' meeting last night.' 'He'll need reviving.'

The Freemasons'
Tavern, Great
Queen Street, in
1803

During the second half of the eighteenth century the Freemasons in the capital decided that they needed a proper hall of their own. They bought a neo-classical house on Great Queen Street near Lincoln's Inn Fields in 1775 with room at the back to build a temple. The front was let to a Brother Luke Reilly as the Freemasons' Tavern and Coffee House. He was allowed to put up a sign with the Freemason's Arms and the motto '*Vide, Audi, Tace*' which was later taken over by the United Grand Lodge. The tavern was rebuilt and extended in 1788, and replaced again in 1869. This present building was renamed the Connaught Rooms, Freemasons' Hall after a current Grand Master in 1909, and is now a conference centre. The Victorian redesign made an effort to separate the tavern as much as possible from the temple:

> one of the great objects in building a new Hall being to provide a proper and dignified home for English Freemasonry which should be entirely unconnected with Tavern or Tavern influence.

The tavern had been equipped with a large banqueting hall, a ballroom and numerous assembly rooms. The first meeting of the Football Association took place there in 1863. The present Freemasons' Hall in London, also known as the Masonic Peace Memorial, was built next door in 1926.

All this suggests that Freemasons originally valued inns and taverns for their up to date facilities rather than any symbolic history. By the end of the nineteenth century Masonic Halls became the norm in many British towns and cities. All were extravagantly decorated inside and some even outside, tending to belie any notion that they involved a 'secret society'.

While the Seven Stars is clearly a significant symbol for Freemasons, there is no evidence that it was important in the early history of inns and taverns with that name. Speculative Freemasonry didn't become well established until much later than many of the earliest pubs and hotels that we have encountered. Furthermore, no lodge meetings have ever been recorded as taking place in the known Seven Stars that were available. Therefore masonry in its various forms is unlikely to have had anything to do with the origins of the name. There are pub names that have masonic associations. The Mason's Arms seems an obvious one but according to Lillywhite it was not found prior to the eighteenth century. The Compass and the Compasses may be another. It is possible that preservation of the name of Seven Stars during the eighteenth and nineteenth centuries and its spread out of the original area of the south-west and the West Midlands could have been influenced by masonic loyalties. The highly decorated Seven Stars on Ashton Old Road, Manchester, with its stars and grapes, might have been a Masonic hotel.

One fact that most Freemasons, with their Neoplatonic and astrological leanings, *are* quite certain about is that their seven stars are the Seven Stars of Taurus, better known as the Pleiades.

Overleaf:
The Masonic
Hall, St Austell

155

THE SOLAR SYSTEM

Nowadays, what with street lighting, televisions, computers screens and all the other night lights and distractions of the modern world, most people have lost sight of the night sky and the wonder that can be engendered by a clear view of the constellations and planets. In the past things were different. The stars were available to everybody, although people may have interpreted them in many different ways. For most of the last 3,000 years educated observers have been convinced that there were seven heavenly bodies making up our solar system: the sun, the moon and five planets. They stood out as being brighter and moved in complex ways against the background of the fixed stars. Before that, in Western Asia and Europe the most prominent of these bodies, the sun, the moon and the planet Venus, were regarded as deities that controlled the ways of the world and demanded veneration.

For millennia human beings have gazed at the night sky and made up stories about the shapes and movements that they saw there, more often than not believing that these characters had a life of their own which mirrored events here on earth. Much of the lore and mythology that was associated with these observations originated before any physical means of recording them was available. They were part of an oral culture which became embedded in stories that were imaginative and indirect. Where these have survived into the modern world they can be difficult to interpret correctly because cultural knowledge and values have changed a great deal from the time of their origin. Detached from their early belief systems, the stories have become altered and embroidered in ways that the original tellers would not have recognised.

The broad description of the night sky and its constellations that is recognised by modern astronomers was laid down by Greek observers in the second half of the first millennium BC. Eudoxus of Cnidus (BC 409-356) is generally credited with the first European systemisation of astronomical knowledge. He is thought to have built a celestial globe showing the constellations, although the first surviving example of such an object is from the Roman period. Eudoxus' conclusions were transmitted to the modern world through the poetry of writers like Aratus (BC 271-13) and the first handbook of astronomy, the *Almagest* of Ptolemy of Alexandria from the second century AD. These ideas were taken up by Arab astronomers at the end of the millennium who provided many of the star names that we now use. In turn, this knowledge was transmitted to Western Europe during the Middle Ages along with subjects such as astrology and alchemy.

However, this simple looking sequence is misleading. When it came to naming constellations and asterisms, early observers had access to thousands of years of their own oral traditions which they selected from. Every local area and cult would have had its own stories about the night sky. Furthermore, the Greek world, although dominating later European culture, was in many ways a sideshow to the older great civilisations of Egypt and Mesopotamia where star lore and celestial observations were a fundamental part of religious culture and which provided many of the systematic observations which later Greek astronomers used. Much of these civilisations' stellar lore and mythology was entirely different. Despite this, there may have been some ideas about the stars that were so ancient that they subsequently appeared in similar forms in many otherwise different cultures.

It is obvious from even a casual glance that stars are not distributed randomly across the sky. This results from two main patterns: the flat, spiral disc of our galaxy which we see side on and which forms the Milky Way; and the local arm of the galaxy which we are in and which means many of the brighter stars cluster around the axis of the same Milky Way. Stars vary in their intrinsic brightness and their distance from us but they appear to the human eye as if projected onto a celestial sphere. Those that are close together seem to form shapes which people in the past have interpreted as real objects in the sky. The constellations created by such patterns have been seen differently by different civilisations. Those of ancient China were almost totally different from those seen in the West. In Western Asia different cultures had their own constellations which evolved over time.

Despite this, some shapes must have been defined at an early stage in human development and were common to the worlds of Egypt and Mesopotamia, and later to Europe. For instance, all these cultures have seen the stars of Leo as a lion, those of Taurus as a bull and those of Orion as a giant human figure with a small head (or even no head at all). Conversely, the Greeks chose to see the stars of Pegasus as a horse with which they were familiar from the central steppe peoples to the north-east whereas the older Mediterranean cultures had never seen horses and viewed the large square of stars in the middle of this constellation as, variously, a field, a temple, a giant turtle or a hippopotamus.

The stars themselves form a largely fixed tapestry which regularly traverses the sky from east to west in the northern hemisphere. In front of them are seven heavenly bodies that have their own characteristic movements. The sun and the moon would have been visible to people from the beginning of human consciousness and the major planets Venus, Mars, Jupiter and Saturn are easily observable during the twilight hours before the main stars appear and similarly just before dawn. Mercury is more difficult to see. Observational records of Venus have been found on cuneiform tablets from Mesopotamia

The moon, Venus and Jupiter near conjunction in the western Sky an hour after sunset, before the background stars become visible

which date to around BC 700 but stories of Venus as the Evening and Morning Stars go back to the earliest Sumerian mythology of the third millennium.

Sumerian was the first human written language, inscribed in a wedge-shaped script (cuneiform) on clay tablets, before being replaced by Akkadian during the second millennium. Many of the tablets that have been recovered and translated date to around BC 1750. Several mythic stories have been reconstructed from them concerning the Goddess Inana and her brother or lover Dumuzid. One of these has been called by modern scholars *Inana's Descent into the Underworld*.

Inana has a compulsion but no explicit reason to visit the underworld. She tells her attendant Ninshuburu that if she is not back after three days Ninshuburu should visit the high gods to demand that they engineer the goddess's return. She then travels to the east until she gets to the gates of the underworld. Here she is successively stripped of all her regalia, turban, beads, pectoral, golden ring, lapiz lazuli rod and divine robe. Finally she is rendered into an emaciated corpse and hung on a hook. When she fails to return, Ninshuburu visits the high gods in turn but they refuse to do anything. Finally Enki, one of the three great gods, agrees to create some fly-like spirits from the dirt under his fingernails and they flit into the underworld and bring Inana back with the agreement that a substitute will be found to replace her. When she gets back Inana is enraged that her husband Dumuzid did not make any efforts to save her so he is nominated as the substitute and is dragged off to the underworld after his limbs have been transformed into snakes by the sun god Utu.[1]

It is easy to be distracted by the anthropomorphic detail in a story like this but it is clearly about the appearance and movements of the planet Venus. The planet is invisible for about two and a half months at superior conjunction when it is on the far side of the sun. It then appears in the west as the Evening Star and moves eastwards against the background stars for about six months, getting nearer the Earth and appearing brighter. It reaches a stationary point in the sky and then moves westwards for about a month. Beyond this point it is side on to the sun and only lit on one hemisphere. As it approaches us the lit portion gets narrower until it appears as a very thin crescent. Then, at inferior conjunction, it passes the sun again and disappears for a few days before reappearing in the eastern sky as the Morning Star. The movements are then reversed until the whole synodic period of about twenty-one months is completed.

As the brightest planet in the night sky, Venus was an important player in early Middle Eastern religion and appears under a variety of names in different cultures, such as Ishtar and Astarte. Her consort also appears as Tamuz in the Old Testament. In later Babylonian times important omens were derived from the appearances and disappearances of Venus at inferior conjunction. Early rising in the east meant the King would have a long life, late rising that he would soon die. Early setting or late rising of the planet were both regarded as unfavourable, from which we can conclude that a very short absence of the goddess was the best sign. Data on the earliest cuneiform tablet recording the sightings of Venus show disappearances varying from three to twenty days. The relation of the former to the myth is unlikely to be an astronomical coincidence. It would show the goddess's ideal, unconstrained state, with longer periods denoting some malicious outside intervention or, in Babylonian times, her increasing displeasure. As the planet approaches conjunction it starts to be eclipsed and becomes a thin crescent. This is not generally seen by the casual observer but would have been visible to a committed sky watcher with good eyesight. This is the corpse of the goddess, stripped of many of its visual attributes.

The myth must come from an era when people still did not completely connect the Evening and Morning Stars, giving one a female personality and the other a male one. The latter is her husband Dumuzid who is chosen to replace her and who initially, when partially eclipsed in the crescent, has a snake's arms and feet. There were a number of variants of this tradition surrounding Venus but its bisexuality was still recognised in

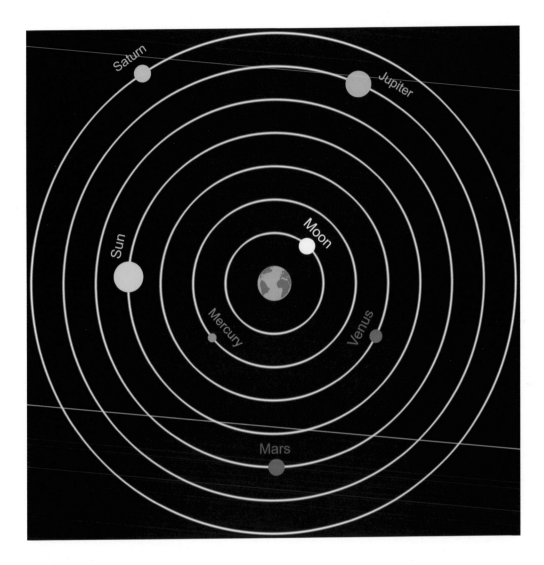

The Solar System according to Ptolemy with the seven heavenly bodies in their crystal spheres

the late Babylonian and Assyrian periods. In some versions Inana was the initiator of the story but the two stars become Dumuzid and his sister. There are later Akkadian versions of the myth about Ishtar. These are fragmented and the story line is more obscure but a comment in Ezekiel about the worship of Tamuz shows that the disappearance of the planet in its male form was still greeted by ritual lamentations in Babylon as late as the sixth century.

It is difficult to say for certain when observers in the Middle East realised that the Evening and Morning Stars were different aspects of the same object. It may have been as late as the end of the second millennium. The classical Greeks seem to have thought it was it was a relatively recent discovery and variously ascribed it to Pythagoras or the sixth century natural philosopher Parmenides. Without this realisation there could not have been a tradition of seven heavenly bodies. However, by the time of Ptolemy we have a fully functional sevenfold geometric theory of the movements of the sun, the moon and the five planets as then known (Uranus, Neptune and Pluto were not discovered until after the eighteenth century of our era). This involved seven crystal spheres surrounding the earth within which the planets had their own circular motions needed to account for their complex movements forward and back across the sky. This was the dominant model of the solar system up until the time of Copernicus and Kepler from the sixteenth century onwards when astronomers began to accept that the earth moved about the sun instead of the other way round. Up until then those with a religious bent to their philosophy saw this as yet another example of the numerical design of creation and the importance of seven in the overall scheme of things. The modern view of astronomy stirred up these by now traditional ideas:

> For heaven
> Is as the book of God before thee set,
> Wherein to read his wondrous works, and learn
> His seasons, hours, days, or months, or years.
> This to attain whether heaven move or earth,
> Imports not, if thou reckon right.
> Hereafter, when they come to model heaven
> And calculate the stars, how they will wield
> The mighty frame, how built, unbuild, contrive,
> To save appearances, how gird the sphere
> With centric and eccentric scribbled o'er,
> Cycle and epicycle, orb in orb.
>   What if the sun
> Be centre to the world and other stars,
> By his attractive virtue and their own
> Incite, dance about him various rounds!
> Their wandering course, now high, now low, then hid,
> Progressive, retrograde, or standing still,
> In six thou seest: and what if seven to these,
> The planet Earth, so steadfast though she seem,
> Insensibly three different motions move?
>   Milton, *Paradise Lost* (1667)

Milton was aware that the Copernican heliocentric view of the solar system reduced the number of circles to six, one of which contained the Earth with the moon orbiting about it. Therefore, in strict terms, by the middle of the sixteenth century the idea of the solar system as seven stars had become redundant. How far this penetrated down through the general population is less clear. It certainly met with resistance from those committed to astrology whose theory was firmly based on the knowledge available to the Greeks, Romans and Arabs. It also became an issue for the Catholic Church during the Counter-Reformation as a reaction to the observations of Galileo that the outer planets were physical bodies like the earth rather than ethereal supralunary spheres subject only to divine action. None of these ideas was really new. During the fifth century BC the Greek philosopher Anaxagoras is said to have only just escaped from Athens with his life after suggesting that the sun was a red-hot stone and the moon was made from the same material as the earth.

It is difficult to believe that these relatively complex ideas originating in classical theories of astronomy had much influence on the minds of people who named inns and taverns during the Middle Ages. Obviously there were hostelries from the earliest times that were named after the sun and moon. There is a record of a 'le Sonne on the Hoop' in the City of London (in West Cheap) from 1390. The sun sign was particularly common in the seventeenth century. In 1636, John Taylor, the Water Poet, wrote:

> The Grape is ripened with bright Phoebus shine
> Which shewes that at the Sun there is good Wine:
> Beware of being Sun-burnt e're thou goe
> Drink civilly, make not they friend they foe.

The Moon as a sign in its own right has been very rare, although there are plenty of Half Moons. Samuel Butler asked in 1651:

> Tell me but what's the natural cause
> Why on a sign no painter draws
> The full moon never, but the half?

The Dutch painter David Teniers the Younger produced at least two paintings around 1660 of peasants celebrating outside an inn with the sign of the new moon, one of them surmounted by a *krug*. Significantly, there have been a few Moon and Seven Stars and there is still a pub called the Half Moon and Seven Stars in Preston, just outside Canterbury. This would be a contradiction if the seven stars were the heavenly bodies.

163

Similar images of a crescent moon and seven stars are known from Roman coins. The emperor Septimius Severus issued several series of *denarii* around AD 200 with this image on the reverse, as did Hadrian around 120. The significance of these symbols for the Romans is still unclear, although in the case of Severus the seven stars could have been a pun on his first name, the Latin for seventh being *septimus*. However, we know from the Roman historian Cassius Dio that Severus was fixated on astrology. He had the ceilings of his palace painted with stars, except for those relating to his personal horoscope which were scrambled in some way. He was born on the 11 April, near to the spring equinox. Severus was in Britain for the last three years of his reign so these coins would have been familiar to people. He planned to expand the Empire by conquering the whole of Scotland. When the Caledonians fought back he decided to exterminate them all but succumbed to gout and died in York.

A silver denarius of the emperor Septimius Severus from AD 194

Few planets have appeared on English inn signs. One pub in Portsmouth in the nineteenth century was called the Morning Star, an evident reference to Venus. Another seems to be Mercury, based on the figure in classical mythology rather than astronomy. According to Larwood and Hotton, he was used to indicate that post-horses were available. To the Greeks and Romans Mercury was the Messenger of the Gods because it is the fastest mover and has the largest orbital eccentricity of the visible planets in the sky, crossing the orbits of all the others. Mercifully, the new planets, Saturn, Uranus and Pluto, have never appeared on inn signs so we are spared ribald comments such as 'See you at Uranus'.

There is therefore little reason to believe that the Seven Stars has ever had anything to do with the seven heavenly spheres of the of the classical solar system, however popular this idea may have been with astronomers and astrologers before Copernicus came along to upset the apple cart and tell us that the Earth revolved around the sun rather than the other way round.

At the Golden Sun *in* Wurtemburg

THE PLOUGH

It seems unlikely that the mundane subject of inn signs was at the forefront of debates about the nature of the cosmos. Added to that, based on casual observation, most ordinary people would have regarded the sun and moon as distinct from the rest of the starry sky even if they knew much about the planets. Other, more convincing candidates exist for seven stars in the sky. The most obvious of these is the Plough, or Big Dipper as the Americans like to call it.

For the Greeks this asterism was part of the constellation of Ursa Major, the Great Bear. While the Plough is evident to any observer in the northern hemisphere, the Great Bear is a rambling constellation that is not immediately visible to the eye. The Greeks could have had ulterior motives for calling this a bear. The hunting goddess Artemis, said to be the ancestor of the Arcadians from the most primitive area of Greece, may have originated as a bear cult. Her priests were called 'bears' and young girls in her service were known as 'little bears' in Attic parts of the country. This was adapted to form the myth of Callisto who was translated to the heavens by a jealous Juno as a bear after some hanky-panky with Zeus. Aristotle suggested these stars had been called the Bear because this was the only animal that could have got that far north.

An alternative idea is that the Greeks borrowed the name from Mesopotamia where the seven stars of the Plough asterism were called the Wagon which was *eriqqu* in Akkadian. They managed to mistranslate this as *arktos* meaning 'bear' in Greek. Anglo-Saxon intellectuals of the tenth century used the Greek names for the stars but said that unlettered people called it Charles' Wain. This agrees with Germanic culture where the asterism was widely called the Wagon (*Wagen*). The name of Plough for these seven stars is first recorded in English by Thomas Fale in his *Horologiographia,* published in London in 1593. He says it is a name used by 'countrymen'.[1]

Even worse, the Greeks called the smaller seven-star constellation next door Ursa Minor, the Little Bear. Seeing this as an animal means lumbering it with a tail that is nearly as long as its body, something uncharacteristic of any bear. It is more realistically seen as a dog. That some Greeks followed the Phoenicians and called the Pole Star at the end of its tail *kynosoura* or the Dog's Tail suggests that this was the case. In this context the seven stars of the Plough can become a large, long tailed fox which at this period in history, due to precession, would have been seen as being chased round the celestial pole by the dog in circles for ever, thus leading to the myth of the Teumessian Vixen.[2] Some later commentators tried to correct the tail problem by suggesting that the tail stars were really the Bear's young following it in a line.

*Due to a wobble
in the earth's axis
which alters over a
cycle of 26,000 years,
known as precession,
the northern stars
seem to change their
positions relative to
the celestial pole over
the ages*

*5000 years ago
the 'Pole Star' was
Thuban in the
constellation of
Draco*

*3000 years ago there
was no clear Pole Star
and the asterism of
the Plough (the large
rectangle and tail on
the right) and the
constellation of the
Little Bear or Ursa
Minor (the smaller
rectangle and tail)
seeemed to chase
each other around the
celestial pole*

*Nowadays, the Pole
Star is Polaris at
the end of the tail of
the Little Bear, also
known to the ancient
Greeks as* kynosoura
or the Dog's Tail

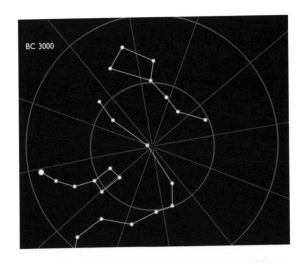

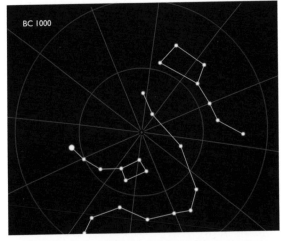

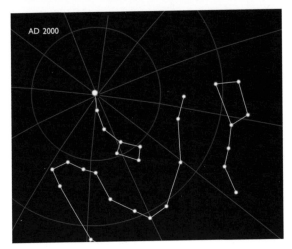

However this may have been, the seven stars of the Plough are a distinctive feature of the northern sky in their own right. Being circumpolar, they are visible throughout the year in the northern hemisphere and have been singled out as special by most cultures. Even the Chinese, whose constellations are nearly all at variance with those of the West, recognised the form. They called it *pih tow*, the Northern Bushel or Northern Measure or even just *tseih sing*, the Seven Stars.[3]

As a name for a pub, the Plough (or Plow) is ambiguous in the sense that it is more likely to refer to agricultural machinery rather than any grouping of stars. A number of inns have been called the Plough and Harrow, Plough and Furrow, Plough and Flail or the Plough and Horses, which convincingly excludes any reference to stars. According to Lillywhite, the name only goes back to the sixteenth century. His earliest record is of an Old Plough Inn at Kensal Green in north-west London, with a building dating to 1500. A number of present Plough Inns claim an ancestry back to the seventeenth century. The Plough Inn in Sittingbourne, Kent, is in a building said to date from 1260 but it was previously a blacksmiths. The Plough Inn in Norwood Green, once in Middlesex but now in outer London, has a building which is said to date from the 1200s but it only became an inn in the seventeenth century. The most northerly Plough in Britain is Scottish and is in Rosemarkie on the Black Isle. It claims to have been first put up in 1691, although the present building dates from 1907.

A minority of modern Plough Inns use the seven stars from Ursa Major as a sign. Most have a traditional plough or a horse and plough. Some modern Seven Stars use the same star sign but we know from Manchester, Bristol, Exeter, Holborn, Knowl Hill and old commentators that the original Seven Stars symbol was a circle of six stars with a seventh in the middle. The Plough, Plough Inn, Olde Plough Inn, Plough Hotel and Plough Tavern are common pub names and are found over most of the UK mainland, far more widely than the Seven Stars. Their distribution is different from that of the Seven Stars. There is a concentration in the Central and East Midlands and the south-east. A good number can be found in East Anglia and Lincolnshire where Seven Stars are largely absent. This would suggest that the Plough has a natural connection with eastern arable farming areas (as one might suspect).

The overlap between the two sets of signs can be attributed to 'symbolism creep' in an age when the original meanings of the images were becoming less relevant and the names of pubs were assigned in a more random manner. This confusion has apparently occurred within the same premises. The Seven Stars in Derby was mentioned in the *Derby Mercury* of August 1775 as 'the Seven Stars otherwise the Plough' which adds to the muddle about its origin. There are Ploughs in the middle of cities such as a Victorian pub in Museum Street near to the British Museum in London. This used to have a star

The modern distribution of pubs and hotels called the Seven Stars on the left, and those called the Plough on the right

sign outside but now has a picture of a horse and plough. It is as far as it is possible to get from an agricultural background. In 1636 John Taylor, the Water Poet, noted the fact that not all Ploughs are in the countryside:

> There's many goes to Plough and does not know,
> Where Corne (upon the ground, or trees) do grow:
> Beware therefore, and looke before thou leape
> And Plough and sow no faster than thou Reape.

Despite these overlaps, however, the evidence suggests that the Seven Stars and the Ploughs were originally two distinct groups of inns with independent histories.

All the northern constellations have been used for navigation, probably for as long as people have travelled. The most directly northern ones have varied in use over the

The most northerly Plough of the British Isles in Rosemarkie, Ross and Cromarty, first built in 1691

millennia due to precession in the earth's axis. This is a wobble with a period of 26,000 years which means that different constellations have coincided with the celestial pole over the centuries. Around BC 3000, during the time of the early Egyptian civilisations, the North Star was Thuban in the constellation of Draco. Around BC 1000 there was no bright northern star and the two bears revolved around at equal distances from the pole. Aratus was a Greek poet who wrote a long poem about astronomy, the *Phaenomena*, during the third century BC. In this he tells us that the Achaeans (the Greeks of the Peloponnese) used the Great Bear for navigation whereas the Phoenicians from Sidon used the Little Bear.

One would expect, therefore, that if the Seven Stars referred to the stars of the Plough it would be a common name for inns and taverns in ports which catered to sailors. We have seen that Bristol (no doubt an important port, although mainly for slavery) had nine Seven Stars around 1760. Portsmouth has been a naval centre since Tudor times and as such has long had a reputation for fostering drinking establishments of all kinds. Many of these were at the lower end of the social scale and attracted gaming and prostitution, something which concerned the local authorities from the eighteenth century onwards and encouraged them to keep records. In 1869 the number of licensed premises in the city peaked at 897.[4] Local historians have tried to identify as many of these as possible. There was the Polar Star, the Morning Star, the Half Moon, the Blue Anchor, the Ship, the Mermaid, the Mayflower, the Hearts of Oak and the Lord Nelson to pick just a few. None of them was called the Seven Stars. The nearest surviving Seven Stars in Hampshire is way inland, just outside Petersfield. This suggests that such a name was not one with a navigational or maritime background that would have appealed to ordinary sailors.

THE SEVEN STARS OF TAURUS

Three to four hundred years ago there were several inns and taverns in England called the Fox and Seven Stars. The Seven Stars in Canterbury was one of these. In the seventeenth century it was named in licensing returns as just the Seven Stars, but during the eighteenth and nineteenth centuries it appeared in leet court records and property advertisements as the Fox and Seven Stars. The first part has now been dropped again from its name. There was another in London which excited opinion among the capital's literati. Coffee house journals and the *Gentlemen's Magazine* were supplied with articles and poems ridiculing the names of inns and taverns for which the writers could find no meaning or precedent. One of the first of these was by Joseph Addison who published 'a letter' (effectively to himself since he was the editor) in *The Spectator* in April 1711:

> My first Task, therefore, should be, like that of Hercules, to clear the City from Monsters. In the second Place, I would forbid, that Creatures of jarring and incongruous Natures should be joined together in the same Sign; such as the Bell and the Neats-tongue, the Dog and Gridiron. The Fox and Goose may be supposed to have met, but what has the Fox and the Seven Stars to do together? and when did the Lamb and Dolphin ever meet, except upon a Sign-Post?

T.I.M. Forster published a poem in the *Perrenial Calendar, and Companion to the Almanac* in 1824 which went onto the subject in greater depth:

> To London let us hie to see
> The signs and shows that there may be,
> The Lions in the Tower, and
> The Beasts at Pidcock's in the Strand,
> Fish Markets and Bookseller's stalls,
> The splendid Shops where Commerce shines,
> And above all the comic Signs
> Of creatures coupled, which to us
> Seem monstrous strange incongruous!
> For when did Lamb and Dolphin meet
> Except on signposts in the street?
> The fiery dangers that environ

A Goose perhaps, may be Gridiron;
But who did ever know, I say,
A Cat that could on Bagpipes play;
Who robbed old Taurus for a hoax;
And gave the Seven Stars to the Fox;
Or loaded Phoebus' flaming car
With a Whalebone in the air;
Bell and Savage, Bull and Gate,
The Fish and Fly his wonted bate,
And the Spread Eagle like a tether
Of two winged Eagles stitched together?
Whoe'er saw such a had me doddy
A Swan with Two Necks to one body?
And other drolleries there are
Too many to be counted here.
Three Sugar loaves where sweets are vended;
At Pawnbrokers Three Balls suspended,
The golden Grape of Raisins shine
Where Bacchus sells his Beer and Wine;
The Smoking Boy declares our need
To fill our Pipes with Indian weed.
Besides a hundred fancies more,
The Puss in Boots, and the Blue Boar.
The Lion Golden, Red and White
The Toyshop sign the Flying Kite.
The Fleeting Hare may well alarm her,
At Flying Pigs and Hogs in Armour.
Each Tradesman thus his banner wields,
From Draper's Gardens to Moorfields
Where stands aloft, outopping all,
The Golden Ball on Bedlam Hall.

It is quite clear from this that the Seven Stars here were accepted as the Seven Stars of Taurus, generally known as the Pleiades.

The Pleiades are a curious collection of stars that have taken on a significant role in world mythology and symbolism that seems wildly out of proportion to the cluster's limited visual appearance. Various investigators have explored their names and

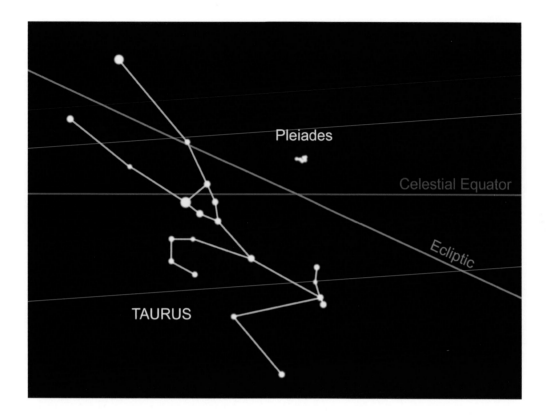

interpretations in cultures ranging from the indigenous people of Australia to those of the Americas. There are a wealth of references to them from the ancient Middle East and classical Europe which have been repeatedly mined by later writers and poets. They have also fuelled the psyches of a full range of fringe theorists and New Age enthusiasts in the nineteenth and twentieth centuries.[1]

To the casual observer the Pleiades seem to be a smudge in the sky above and to the right of the constellation of Taurus. Over the millennia more serious students of astronomy have decided that they consist of seven stars, although people with the best eyesight may be able to distinguish up to a dozen. With a modern telescope hundreds are visible. However, in this as in many others situations, tradition has held sway and seven has become the accepted complement.

Modern interpretations of the Pleiades have been heavily influenced by Greek mythology and astronomy. Ancient authorities of repute such as Homer and Hesiod tell us that there were seven Pleiads, maidens who were subject to the attentions of other gods and eventually immortalised in the sky. They were called Alcyone, Electra, Maia, Merope, Taygeta, Celaeno and Sterope. These can be seen as a lop-sided rosette with Maia in the middle. Some joker later decided to add their mythical father Atlas to the

*The seven
Pleiads and
their father
Atlas*

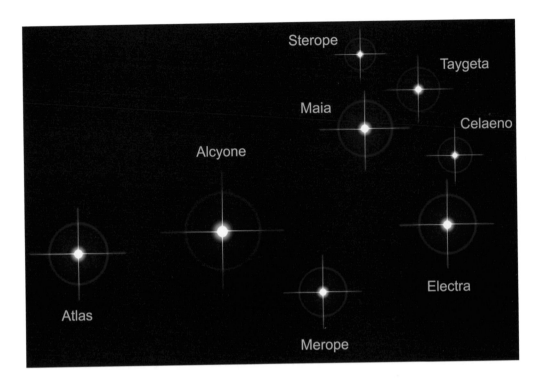

The seven Pleiads and their father Atlas

party so that in these terms the Pleiades consist of eight stars. This inclusion of an eighth star has created a shape which is arranged in a similar way to that of the Plough leading some people to call them the Little Dipper or Wagon, a name that might otherwise be reserved for the Little Bear. However, the Plough covers almost 200 times the area of sky compared to the Pleiades. Despite this, some in the ancient world may have connected the two. The Roman mythographer, Hyginus, tells a story in his *Poetic Astronomy* of a lost Pleiad which crossed the sky and went to live next to the Plough near the Pole in mourning for the destruction of Troy.

Whichever culture it was that actually came to the conclusion that there were seven stars in the Pleiades has been lost in the mists of prehistory. It is said that they are first referred to in copies of literature from the third millennium BC in China. The Nebra Sky Disc is a ritual object from the Bronze Age of Germany dating to about BC 1600. Against the bronze background, now corroded, are gold images of the sun and moon, a crescent that is probably the planet Venus and small, circular stars. Seven of these are arranged in our familiar grouping of six in a circle with a seventh in the middle, much like the original signs for Seven Stars inns. Two sighting bands have been added to the rim of the disc which are generally interpreted as showing the limits of the annual arcs travelled by the rising and setting sun along the horizon.

Some have even claimed to see the Pleiades in one of the cave paintings of a bull at Lascaux in south-west France from the Upper Palaeolithic era, dating to around BC 15000. They are certainly evident on a gold coin from north-east Gaul produced about AD 100. Here their resemblance to seven turds coming from the back of the horse bears a strong resemblance to older Middle Eastern images of the Animal Orchestra, such as that on a limestone plaque from Guzana (Tell Halaf in modern Syria) of about BC 800, although there the image is probably of an ass. This is a relatively late piece but has many resemblances to the images on cylinder seals from the Third Dynasty of Ur dating to the third millennium BC. The Animal Orchestra shows images of musical instrument playing, dancing and drinking. In the Guzana

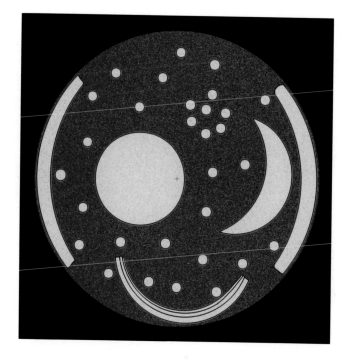

The Nebra Sky Disc that was discovered in Saxony in 1996

piece a reference is made to a more sophisticated method of extracting beer from a brew pot by syphoning. Behind all this though, the inclusion of the seven stars suggests that these images are all fanciful views of the constellations and that these were considered to bear some relationship to brewing beer or, at the very least, to seasonal festivities that involved drinking.

The Sumerian and Akkadian cultures of Mesopotamia from the third to the first millennia BC have provided us with our most detailed knowledge of early Middle Eastern astronomy. Observation of the heavenly bodies was central to their religious culture. The Babylonians and the Assyrians believed that the sun, moon, planets and constellations were gods in the sky. Initially they regarded events such as eclipses as omens which showed the god's state of mind and which had implications for what would happen down here on earth. Efforts to predict when eclipses were likely to occur developed into detailed observations of how the planets and stars moved in relation to each other and led to the development of astrology and, later, scientific astronomy.

A gold coin from the Moselle Valley, France, dated to between BC 150 and 50

An image of the Animal Orchestra carved on a limestone panel from the city of Guzana. Among other things, this shows the siphoning of beer

In this Middle Eastern astronomy the Pleiades played an important role despite their relative obscurity compared to other, brighter celestial phenomena. They were called 'The Stars', ^MULMUL, in Sumerian and *zappu* in Akkadian, the two main literary languages of ancient Mesopotamia written on clay tablets in a cuneiform or wedge-shaped script. Apparently this required no further qualification and Babylonian observers of the heavens were sure that there were seven of them. In later Akkadian they were the *sebet ilani* or *Sebittu*, the Seven Gods. The most famous cuneiform collection of celestial omens and phenomena, MUL.APIN, from around BC 1000, has the emphatic line:

The Stars, the Seven Gods, the Great Gods.[2]

Almost similar wording can be found in another cuneiform astronomical text which some have dated to the sixth millennium. These gods had temples in Nimrud, Khorsabad and Nineveh and were anthropomorphised as tall figures in long robes and cylindrical feathered hats. Each carried an axe, a knife, a bow and a quiver of arrows.[3]

In late Babylonian and Assyrian art the Pleiades also appeared as seven dots or stars, particularly on cylinder seals that were used for certifying clay tablets and pots. The first occurrence of these seven dots is on seals produced by the Mitanni from what is now northern Syria and south-western Turkey during the last half of the second millennium BC. Here they are shown as rosettes with a ring of six stars and another in the middle. In later seals from the Assyrian and Neo-Babylonian period the dots become a parallel row of three pairs with a seventh at the end.[4] Some cuneiform astronomical tablets show them as actual stars. On a few seals the Seven Stars are shown as coequal with the sun, the moon and Venus. One fairly crude Mittanean seal from the second half of the second millennium BC shows the Stars with the sun, the moon, Venus and the constellation of Scorpio. The seasonal opposition of the Pleiades and Scorpio was noted in MUL.APIN:

> The Stars rise and the Scorpion sets, and the Scorpion rises and the Stars set.

The other images, one a giant human figure, a tree and a selection of winged animals, are probably also astral objects.

A late Mittanian image on a cylinder seal from north-west Syria

Another example of a seal image from the thirteenth century BC has a figure of the Assyrian war god Ninurta standing on a plinth or ziggurat holding a sceptre and a lightning bundle. In front of him is a priestess with an incense burner and an offering table. The four astral symbols are the sun, crescent moon, an Omega sign which is an alternative figuration for the planet Venus, and the Seven Stars of the Pleiades. An incised tablet from the Seleucid period (fourth century BC) shows the Pleiades as actual stars together with an image of a bull. In between is a Herculean figure in a disc holding a lion by the tail. This imagery was used quite widely in the Middle East of the first

The image on a late Assyrian Style cylinder seal from Tyre

The engraving on a Seleucid period clay tablet

millennium BC as a symbol for a sun god. The bull that is shown has a distinct hump which is characteristic of the zebu breeds that originated in the region of ancient Pakistan.

Where did this singling out of the Pleiades as so important come from? The answer is to be found in the interactions between astral religions and the need for a seasonal calendar. Circumpolar stars, like those of Ursa Major, are visible throughout the year at intermediate latitudes. The rest are hidden behind the sun for part of the year. In the ancient Middle East the most important technique for dating was to observe their reappearance just before dawn along the eastern horizon. Technically this is known as heliacal rising or 'morningfirst'. In the Mesopotamian world, as in that of later Persia, the New Year was celebrated at the Spring Equinox, not at mid-winter as in northern countries. Around BC 1000 the second month of the year was defined by the rising of the Pleiades. As MUL.APIN says:

On the first of Ayaru the Stars become visible.

Accurate dating can be either sidereal: the time of the location of a star at a precise place in the night sky; or solar: the annual movements of the sun from the shortest to the longest day and back. Unfortunately, most early cultures seem to have been more impressed by the big, shiny moon in the sky. Many old calendars were originally based on the phases of the moon's waxing and waning in relation to the background stars. At several removes these are still the origin of our modern months. In Mesopotamia the new month was defined by the first appearance of a new moon while a particular star was rising in the east. The problem with this system is that the number of lunar months does not fit exactly into a solar year so that continual adjustments to the calendar have to be made by interpolating extra days and, in the late Mesopotamian empires, whole extra shortened months into the calendar.

The purpose of precise calendars was more religious than practical so that festivals could be planned at the right times of year and predictions of the Gods actions could be made. Such astrological research finally settled on the sun as more important than the moon and by the seventh century BC a zodiac was developed in Mesopotamia which followed the movements of the sun through twelve equally spaced regions of the stars. Even this did not work out properly, though, because the significant stations of the sun, the summer and winter solstices and the spring and autumn equinoxes (where the ecliptic path of the sun crosses the celestial equator) are affected by precession in the earth's axis. Thus before 3000 years BC the vernal equinox was in the constellation of Gemini, for the next 2000 years it was in Taurus, after BC 1000 it was in Aries and it is now in Pisces. The modern zodiac used by astrologers has had its start fixed at the First Point of Aries.

Before the solar zodiac was invented in the Middle East there is evidence that a lunar zodiac was in use. MUL.APIN has a list of seventeen constellations (one may be missing) with the statement that they are all:

Great Gods that stand in the path of the moon,

and through whose regions the moon passes and whom he touches in a month. The first of these was the Pleiades.[5] Later astrologers in India expanded these lunar mansions or *nakshatras* to twenty-seven or twenty-eight but still retained the Pleiades as a start. This system was followed by Arab astrologers and was probably familiar to many people in the European Middle Ages.

Whether these ideas affected the naming of medieval hostelries is unknown. However, the Half Moon and Seven Stars is known as a London sign from 1650s onward. There is still an old Half Moon and Seven Stars near Canterbury. According to Lillywhite, there were at least ten taverns in London with this name, mainly in the East End. There have been a few Moon and Seven Stars and a Sun, Moon and Seven Stars. All of these may have had an astrological connection rather than anything to do with some of the other explanations that have been put forward which include something to do with Turks, the Huguenots or slang words for coins.

Due to precession, the Pleiades have appeared later in the year over the millennia and have also risen higher into the night sky. They were nearest to the horizon around 9000. By BC 7000 they would have appeared in the east at the spring equinox but whether this was significant or not has been lost in the mists of prehistory. The Pleiades month in Mesopotamia, Ayaru, was written in Akkadian using one of the Sumerian cuneiform signs for Bull, GUD, suggesting that this calendar astronomy was developed during the Age of Taurus. After BC 1000 they were rising in what is our month of May, named by the Romans after the star Maia who they conflated with an ancient Italian Goddess of Spring. The Pleiades reached their zenith between July and August and eventually set in the west during late winter. Despite this prolonged exposure it was mainly their visibility in the morning sky that was of greatest significance to ancient observers.

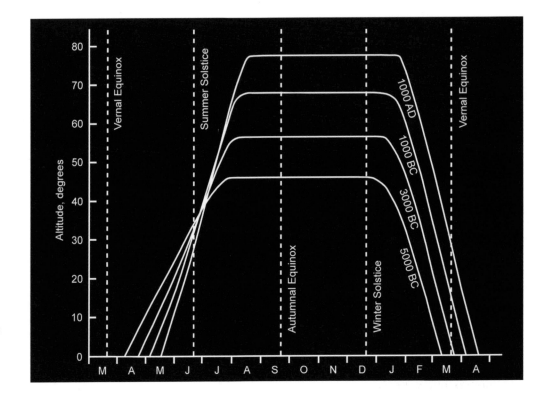

The maximum visible height of the Pleiades in the northern sky throughout the year, and the effects of precession in the earth's axis over the millennia

This seasonal aspect of the Pleiades is probably behind the Lord's reply to Job in the Old Testament about the inexorable divinity of nature:

> Hast thou perceived the breadth of the earth? Declare if thou knowest it all.
> Where is the way where light dwelleth? And as for darkness, where is the place thereof?
> Hast thou entered into the treasures of the snow? Or hast thou seen the treasures of the hail,
> Which I have reserved against the time of trouble, against the day of battle and war?
> By what way is the light parted, which scattereth the east wind upon the earth?
> Who hath divided a watercourse for the overflowing of waters, or a way for the lightning or thunder;
> To cause it to rain on the earth, where no man is; on the wilderness, wherein there is no man;
> To satisfy the desolate and waste ground; and to cause the bud of the tender herb to spring forth?
> Hath the rain a father? or who hath begotten the drops of dew?
> Out of whose womb came the ice? And the hoary frost of heaven, who hath gendered it?
> The waters are hid as with a stone, and the face of the deep is frozen.
> Can'st thou bind the sweet influence of the Pleiades, or loose the hands of Orion?

In contrast to this hymn of pastoralists, the seasonal importance of the Pleiades as a sign for farmers on earth was emphasised by the eighth century BC Greek poet Hesiod in his *Works and Days*:

> When the Pleiades, daughters of Atlas, are rising, begin your harvest, and your ploughing when they are going to set.
> Forty nights and days they are hidden and appear again as the year moves round, when first you sharpen your sickle.
> This is the law of the plains, and of those who live near the sea, and who inhabit rich country, the glens and dingles far from the tossing sea,
> Strip to sow and strip to plough and strip to reap, if you wish to get in all Demeter's fruits in due season, and that each kind may grow in its season.
> Else, afterwards, you may chance to be in want, and go begging to other men's houses, but without avail.

> But when the snail, in early May, climbs up the plants from the earth to escape
> the Pleiades, then it is no longer the season for digging vineyards, but to whet
> your sickles and rouse up your slaves.
> Avoid shady seats and sleeping until dawn in the harvest season, when the sun
> scorches the body.
> Then be busy, and bring home your fruits, getting up early to make your
> livelihood sure.
> For dawn takes away a third part of your work, dawn advances a man on his
> journey and advances him in his work, dawn which appears and sets many men
> on their road, and puts yokes on many oxen.
> But when Orion and Sirius are come into mid-heaven, and rosy-fingered Dawn
> sees Arcturus then cut off all the grape-clusters, Perses, and bring them home.
> Show them to the sun ten days and ten nights: then cover them over for five, and
> on the sixth day draw off into vessels the gifts of joyful Dionysus.
> But when the Pleiades and Hyades and strong Orion begin to set, then
> remember to plough in season: and so the completed year will fitly pass
> beneath the earth.

The Pleiades are not such a prominent formation or point in the sky that they would have been used very much for navigation but the stars have still been connected with the sea. In Germany we are told that some people called them the Sailors Stars (*Schiffahrts Gestirn*).[6] This may be a reflection of Hesiod's description of the their appearance at a time when sailing is possible due to peaceful seas, rather than anything to do with celestial navigation. The Pleiades should be considered when considering taking a sea voyage in October and November:

> But if desire for uncomfortable sea-faring seize you; when the Pleiades plunge into
> the misty sea to escape Orion's rude strength, then truly gales of all kinds rage.
> Then keep ships no longer on the sparkling sea, but bethink you to till the land
> as I bid you. Haul up your ship upon the land and pack it closely with stones all
> round to keep off the power of the winds which blow damply, and draw out the
> bilge-plug so that the rain of heaven may not rot it.
> Put away all the tackle and fittings in your house, and stow the wings of the sea-
> going ship neatly, and hang up the well-shaped rudder over the smoke.
> You yourself wait until the season for sailing is come, and then haul your swift
> ship down to the sea and stow a convenient cargo in it, so that you may bring
> home profit.

Despite their disappearance from the morning sky in autumn the Pleiades are still visible in the west until late winter. The Greeks connected their final disappearance below the horizon with the halcyon days of mid-winter (the breeding time of a mythical kingfisher), a period when the sea became calm for a few weeks. However, it is questionable whether this was of much significance outside the eastern Mediterranean.

In standard Greek mythology the Pleiades were the daughters of Atlas, the large character who held the heavens up on his back. Why this should have been is never explained. One possibility is that in some ancient parallel mythology the huge humanoid constellation of Orion was seen in this way and associated with the nearby cluster of stars. The connection was then ignored by later Greek and Roman poets who had other story lines in mind and only the name remained. Their mother was Pleione, an Oceanid nymph with a fleeting connection with the sea but otherwise of little apparent significance. Each of the Pleiads was given her own name and history. However, this did not consist of much more than consorting (if that is the right word) with one of the senior gods in order to give birth to other gods or heroes.

The brightest star in the group is Alcyone. Despite this, she had a limited profile in Greek mythology. Her role was to bear two obscure sons to the sea god Poseidon. The Arabs were not very impressed by this and called her the Walnut, the Bright One or the Central One. Several of the least bright stars have been called the Lost Pleiad that worried those ancient observers with poorer eyesight who thought there were only six and that the seventh had wandered elsewhere in the heavens as repentance or in shame over something. In the case of Merope, this was because she married a mortal, Sisyphus, the gentleman who had to keep rolling a stone up a hill in Hades for playing tricks on too many gods during his life. Alternatively, the lost Pleiad was Electra who was in mourning for her son Dardanus after the sacking of Troy and who went to live next to the Plough. The most celebrated of the Pleiades in the classical world was Maia, apparently the first born and most beautiful. She was the mother of Hermes after receiving the attentions of Zeus. Hermes was a popular and multi-tasking Greek god with attributes that had probably been merged from many different traditions. However, his main job was as a messenger for the gods. This was almost certainly because he was originally conflated with Mercury, which is the fastest moving and most eccentric of the planets in the night sky. The Romans called him *Mercurius*. They took his mother's name from the Greeks and attached it to an Old Italian fertility goddess. Her festival was celebrated in the middle of the month which they called *mensis Maius*, our May.

All this emphasises the role that the Pleiades played in pre-scientific cultures from many millennia BC up until the end of the Middle Ages. Much of the significance of the Pleiades in the ancient Middle East came from the time of their seasonal appearance and the fact that they were more or less in the path of the moon. It may be that the insistence throughout the ages that there were seven of them was linked to this connection with the moon. From the middle of the first millennium BC predictive astrology and the calendar became more sun-oriented so that the Pleiades slipped from the main stage and became an astronomical sideshow. However, there have always been other traditions in many cultures that were more concerned with their intrinsic appearance and their position in relation to surrounding constellations. These have provided other sources of symbolism from past times when, in the absence of television and street lights, people had more time to stare at the night sky and make up stories and develop beliefs about the stars that they saw there.

STARS AND MONASTERIES

We have already seen how the hexagram or six-pointed star was a symbol for beer in parts of Germany in the Middle Ages and eighteenth century, and is still found to the present day. How is it that such a sign could have become a symbol for drink of any kind?

Obviously in this country the Star, usually the five pointed variety, has been used as the name for many pubs. Which particular star the founders had in mind is debatable. In the Middle Ages the Star of Bethlehem might have seemed a suitable and uncontroversial choice. Stars of all kinds have always been common in heraldry. One was taken up as a crest by the Company of Innholders in 1636. In Europe stars and alcohol have been intimately connected for the last thousand years.

The Star,
Rusper

The fermenting of fruit juice and stewed grain to produce alcoholic drinks was known about long before the start of recorded human history. As mentioned in the Introduction, the requirements of producing beer for celebrations and rituals may have been the spur for the Neolithic Revolution. The principle of distillation was known about throughout the classical world. Aristotle was aware that you could get pure water by heating seawater. However, the fact that you could produce a pure (or, at least, pure-ish) liquid by distilling wine seems to have been discovered by Arab alchemists who gave it the name *al-Kohl*. Surprisingly, this actually means a black eye shadow made from powdered antimony. Based on the refining processes needed to manufacture this, by extension Arab alchemists applied the name to any 'essence' that could be obtained by sublimating or distilling raw materials. One of these was the 'alcohol of wine'. Such knowledge was transmitted to Europe during the Middle Ages where alchemists were impressed by the liquid's preservative properties. They were interested in anything that they considered incorruptible or eternal. Their primary obsessions were with gold and the elixir of everlasting life.

To begin with, distilled alcohol was seen mainly as a medicine. Arnaud de Villeneuve, writing in the twelfth century, said:

> Some people call it Eau de Vie (Water of Life) and this name is remarkably suitable, since it is really a water of immortality. Its virtues are beginning to be recognised, it prolongs life, clears away ill humours, revives the heart and maintains youth.

The emblem of the Carthusian Order, founded by Bruno of Cologne in 1084

Scholars at the Papal court (half of which was then in Avignon due to a split within the Papacy) were experimenting with distilling alcohol during the first half of the fourteenth century as part of their studies in alchemy. The most prominent of these was a Franciscan monk called John of Rupescissa. It may appear strange that a Franciscan who had sworn an oath of poverty should be concerned with manufacturing things like gold and alcohol but his main motivation seems to have been to provide resources for the Church during the tribulations that he thought were about to come with the impending reign of the Antichrist. He made extensive studies of this new 'alcohol of wine'. He was so impressed with the ability of alcohol to preserve perishable materials such as raw meat, that he called it the Fifth Element (*quinta essentia* or quintessence) and wrote a treatise on it around 1350 called *On the Consideration of the Fifth Essence of All Things*.[1] He also found that it could be used for extracting substances from herbs to create medicinally useful tinctures. In time the alcohol content of such tinctures took precedence over the herbs involved, which were chosen more for their bouquet than their medicinal properties. The results were liqueurs such as Benedictine and Chartreuse. These were often still promoted for their health benefits, although some recipes include up to 150 herbs so they were presumably meant to cure everything.

One modern Chartreuse has a label with seven stars on it together with an orb and a cross and the motto: 'The cross stands firm while the world turns upside down'. This is the emblem of the Carthusian monks who produce it. The seven stars here are said to represent St Bruno and his six companions who founded the order in 1084, although the emblem in its present form may only have been used from the sixteenth century. Carthusians from Grande Chartreuse began founding monasteries (Charterhouses) in Britain from 1181. They extended from Somerset to Perth in Scotland.

The idea that everything in nature is composed of various combinations of four elements goes back to the time of the ancient Greeks. The earliest Greek philosophers that we know of argued among themselves about the most important constituents of the natural world. Some said that the element which controlled all action in the cosmos was fire; others thought it might be water. Some were more materialist and said earth was the basis of all matter and hence of everything else. Sometime around BC 440 a Sicilian called Empedocles, while playing around with a water clock, observed that if you put an upturned bucket into water there was something which stopped it from filling up. He added this principle to the other three and established the doctrine of the 'four elements': Earth, Air, Fire and Water. Under the influences of attraction and animosity these four eternal principles came together in various combinations and created everything we see around us. The perfect blend of all four formed the incorruptible metal gold.

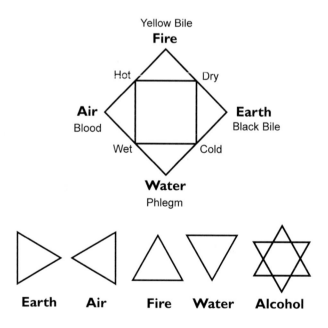

*Opposite left:
Brother Basil
Valentine from
the frontpiece
to a 1717
edition of the*
Chymische
Schrifften

This theory dominated all Middle-Eastern and Western thought about the physical as well as the medical world for the next two thousand years. Later Greek 'atomists' proposed that the cosmos was further subdivided into microscopic particles that clumped together to produce everything but these were still based on the concept of the 'four elements' and this formulation stood the test of time until the scientific revolution of the eighteenth century when the real chemical elements started to be discovered.

The belief that geometry is imbued with metaphysical symbolism goes back at least to the age of Pythagoras. By the Middle Ages it had become the convention to depict the four elements as a diagram with a square within a square, thus creating four triangles all facing in different directions. In this view Fire inevitably goes up and Water goes down. The combination of these two triangles, when overlapped equally, creates a hexagram, the natural sign for the Fifth Element: Fire-Water. This star can be seen in alchemical texts. For instance, a book called *Chymische Schrifften* (Writings on Chemistry) produced in Hamburg in 1717 has a front piece showing a Brother Basil Valentine with some of his apparatus (including a 'philosopher's egg') and a hexagram on the wall next to him. In the landscape behind can be seen a fox and two cockerels, allegorical images for some of the chemicals used in various reactions. These were chosen for their colours and the fact that one, an acid that dissolves gold, 'eats' the other. The acid in question was probably *aqua regia*, a mixture of nitric and hydrochloric acids which is capable of dissolving the 'royal metal'. Here the hexagram may be being used as a symbol for alchemy in general rather than alcohol in particular. It has naturally been suggested that the German beer star is a direct product of this medieval symbolism given the parallel interests of monks in brewing and alchemy, but such an idea is difficult to prove.

By dissolving gold, alchemists could perform various operations on it and supposedly increase the amount in the eventual products. Since this is not, in fact, possible, the more unscrupulous alchemists (or perhaps all of them) would introduce extra precious metals into the brew by sleight of hand in order to impress their clients who would then cough up large sums of money for the recipe.

The books and tracts on alchemy that were written in Latin during the Middle Ages were meant for fellow adepts and used extremely obscure symbolic and allegorical language which is hard to decode nowadays. The alchemists they were meant for had to be literate and fluent in Latin, which meant that most of them were churchmen. Brother Valentine is said to have been a fifteenth century German monk who was the Canon of a Priory in Erfurt. No evidence has been found for the existence of such a person and he may have been a German salt manufacturer called Johann Thölde who published a book under this pseudonym in 1599. He frequently refers to a 'spirit' that could be obtained by distilling wine but since it dissolved a variety of things he thought it was another acid.

Whether Brother Valentine actually existed or not, there is no doubt that alchemy was popular in monasteries, to the extent that Pope John XXII issued a decree condemning it in 1317. This does not seem to have had much effect, as we can tell from Geoffrey Chaucer's *The Canon's Yeoman's Tale* where he lists the people most likely to be involved:

> Perhaps you think that craft is so easy to acquire?
> No, God knows, be he monk or friar,
> Priest or canon, or any other wight,
> Though he sits at his books both day and night
> In learning this precise, elusive lore,
> All is in vain, and, forgive me, there is much more.

*Above:
A medieval
German
image of a
monk stirring
a brew kettle
underneath a
brewer's star*

This is the only chapter of the *Canterbury Tales* that is thought to have been invented entirely by Chaucer. It has been suggested that the story was a result of his being duped at some time by a priest who claimed to be able to manufacture silver, although, being a professional diplomat, he is keen not to condemn the Church as whole:

> But worshipful canons religious,
> Do not think I slander your house,
> Although my tale is about a canon.
> In every order there are some who lie
> And God forbid that all the company
> Should rue just one man's folly.
> To slander you is not my intent,
> But to correct what is amiss I meant,
> This tale is told not only for you
> But also for others; you well know
> That among Christ's apostles twelve
> There was a traitor, Judas himself.
> Then why should the rest be blamed
> That guiltless were? For you I say the same,
> Save only this, if you will hear me,
> If there's any Judas in your party,
> Kick him out right smartly,
> Lest you be shamed and lost thereby,
> And be not displeased I pray,
> But listen to what I have to say.

Such priests were well versed in the Neoplatonist beliefs of the day, another inheritance from the eastern and classical worlds. By the third or fourth centuries AD these had become encapsulated in what was known as Hermetic Philosophy from a work called the *Hermetica*. This was a collection based on older Greek and Middle Eastern texts which was probably written in Alexandria and thus considered to have been founded on ancient Egyptian wisdom. Brother Valentine was described as a Hermetic Philosopher as well as an Alchemist. The reference is to *Hermes Trismegestus* (the 'Thrice Greatest'), a synthesis of the Greek God Hermes, generally identified with the planet Mercury, the messenger of gods, and the Egyptian god of knowledge and writing Thoth. Translations of the Greek text had a profound effect all over Europe and were considered to be more important than the works of Plato.

The Greek philosopher Plato had devised a centralised view of the Cosmos in which all knowledge derived from a single mind. The ideas in this mind diffused into the physical world to create real objects which were an imperfect representation of the ideal form that created them. The source of this perfection was 'out there somewhere' and many came to associate it with the celestial world they could see in the heavens which seemed to exist in an eternal state and which progressed in circles, the perfect, endless form. The more mystical branches of this philosophy saw the stars as the home of human souls, the essential spark from the creator which had been allied with mundane materials to create humans in the first place. At death each soul returned to be a star in the heavens. People die because they cannot connect their end to their beginning but by becoming a star they achieve circular motion which is endless. Over the previous thousand years the Babylonians had devised an extensive system of religious divination based on the appearance and movements of the heavenly bodies and this developed into predictive astrology which connected events here on earth with the state of the sun, moon, stars and planets. In Neoplatonism all these aspects became welded together into a general theory of knowledge which connected alchemy, astrology and medicine together with a liberal sprinkling of what we would consider magic and superstition. This was the 'Science' of the Middle Ages with which Chaucer was familiar:

> I will tell you as was taught to me,
> The four spirits, and the bodies seven,
> By order, as I often heard my lord assert.
> The first spirit is quicksilver called,
> The second orpiment, the third is known,
> As sal ammoniac, and the fourth brimstone.
>
> The seven bodies are here laid down,
> Gold is the Sun, and silver the Moon,
> Mars is iron and Mercury quicksilver,
> Saturn is lead and tin is Jupiter,
> And, on my father's name,
> Venus is copper just the same.

The human world was a 'microcosm', a miniature reflection of the greater universe, the 'macrocosm', with which it was intimately connected at all levels. The connections with the stars are made clear from some passages in the *Hermetica*, as translated by Walter Scott in 1924:

And the fiery substance was articulated, with the gods therein; and heaven appeared, with its seven spheres, and the gods, visible in starry forms, with all their constellations. And heaven revolved, and began to run its circling course, riding upon the divine air.

And God ordained the births of men, and bade mankind increase and multiply abundantly. And he implants each soul in flesh by means of the gods who circle in the heavens.

And it is the lot of men to live their lives and pass away according to the destiny of the gods who circle in the heavens, and to be resolved into the elements.

God is the Maker of all things, and makes all things like unto himself; but though good when first made, they can be corrupted when the cosmic force works on them; for the movement of the Cosmos varies the birth of things, and gives them this or that quality; it fouls with evil the births of some things, and purifies with good the births of others.

For nature tempers the composition of the body according to the influence of the stars; and the soul, taking over the body as made by nature, thereupon confers life on the body which nature has made. The tempering of bodies is of three kinds, namely, that in which the hot element preponderates, that in which the cold element preponderates, and that in which is the mean; and nature tempers them according to the star or planet which has got control over the mixing of these elements.

On a far greater scale than its occasional lapses into alchemy, the European monastic system was intimately connected with alcohol through brewing and viniculture of all kinds. The tradition of the sacramental use of wine goes back as far as the New Testament's description of the Last Supper, itself modelled on the Jewish Feast of Passover. This is described in three of the Gospels, of which Luke 22: 13-20 is the most explicit:

And they went, and found as he had said unto them: and they made ready the passover.

And when the hour was come, he sat down, and the twelve apostles with him.

And he said unto them, With desire I have desired to eat this passover with you before I suffer:

For I say unto you I will not any more eat thereof, until it be fulfilled in the Kingdom of God.

And he took the cup, and gave thanks, and said, Take this, and
divide it among yourselves:

For I say unto you, I will not drink of the fruit of the vine, until
the Kingdom of God shall come.

And he took bread, and gave thanks, and brake it, and gave unto
them, saying, This is my body which is given for you: this do
in remembrance of me.

Likewise also the cup after supper, saying, This cup is the new
testament in my blood, which is shed for you.

Even the fourth, St. John, connects Jesus with wine:

I am the true vine, and my Father is the husbandman.

Every branch in me that beareth not fruit he taketh away: and every branch
that beareth fruit, he purgeth it, that it may bring forth more fruit.

John 15: 1-2.

The communal meal that is described became a model for one of the primary celebrations of Christianity, the Eucharist. While this may initially have been just a real supper, by the thirteenth century the symbolism involved had taken over from the practice and many claimed that the bread and wine had become disembodied from their objective existence and been metamorphosed into metaphysical entities that were literally the flesh and blood of Christ. This was the Doctrine of Transubstantiation. Exactly how this happened was difficult to explain in the real world and various other theories such as consubstantiation, transfinalisation, transfunctionalisation and transsignification have since muddied this wine.

The importance of wine to Christianity is reflected in a fifteenth century German pastry mould which shows Jesus treading grapes. Interestingly, He is surrounded by numerous stars, although they have no obvious pattern. Obviously the practice of treading grapes goes back much further than the time of Jesus. In the classical world it was the preserve of the Greek and Roman gods Dionysos and Bacchus. People treading grapes in the seventh century were still wearing the masks of satyrs and shouting the names of Dionysos until the Council of Constantinople intervened in 691 and made them shout *kyrie eleison* instead.[2] As in other aspects of Christianity, it is likely that many rituals and symbols associated with these more ancient gods were subsumed into the new religion and in time were accepted as natural and legitimate because everybody had forgotten their origins. The cult of Dionysos had itself been introduced into Greece

The image on a terracotta pastry mould from the Rhineland around 1450

during the first half of the first millennium BC and came from countries further to the east or south where the cultivation of grapes first began.

Monasticism was not an original part of Christianity. For the first couple of centuries after the death of Christ, Christians met together in worshipping groups to prepare themselves for the Second Coming. While a pagan Roman Empire was in operation anybody who wanted a shortcut to the everlasting could choose martyrdom. However, by the fourth century AD it started to become clear that the Second Coming was on hold. The reason for this could only be because of the sinfulness of the human race. Therefore more drastic measures were needed to intercede with the Almighty. Groups that withdrew from society and dedicated themselves to an ascetic, prayerful life started to appear in Egypt and the fashion travelled up the eastern Mediterranean to Syria. Most of these lived in the desert and survived on a few dates a week. The first monasteries in Europe were started in 413 around Marseille and by the end of the century had extended up into Germany.

To provide a consistent code of practice for these new institutions, the Abbot of Monte Cassino in central Italy, Benedict of Nursia, established a set of rules around 540 which have defined Western monasticism ever since. These were more humane and practical than the habits in the Eastern churches. The role of each member of the community was defined and allowance made for adequate sleep, nutrition and physical labour. Each monk should be allocated a pound of bread and around a quarter of a litre of wine a day (abstinence was still considered as meritorious but not essential). Guests should be welcomed 'as Christ himself' and given board and lodging but should be kept separate from the main congregation. One or two monks must be directed to cater for them and a separate kitchen maintained for their needs. They should only be turned away if they proved ungodly and disruptive.

The first vineyards in northern Europe were planted by Greek and Roman émigrés who, among others things, sold the wine to their barbarian neighbours as a luxury. The liturgical necessity for wine in the Catholic Church meant that the early monasteries were keen to grow their own, although they may also have received some as a gift from other landowners. As early as the sixth century the Benedictines had become active wine growers. By the end of the millennium many monasteries had become rich and powerful institutions which could command large land holdings of their own. One of the prime wine growing regions of France, Burgundy, belonged to the local Benedictine and Cistercian abbeys from the twelfth century up until the time of the French Revolution. Various saints were given the reputation of creating or defending vineyards: St Martin is supposed to have used his donkey to prune vines in the Loire Valley, St Germain was responsible for them among the Seine, St Remi for Reims and St Didier in Quercy.

Making wine (whatever oenophiles may say) is a relatively primitive process and is a by-product of the decomposition of fruit. It remained mysterious until the investigations of Louis Pasteur in the nineteenth century. By contrast, brewing good beer is more akin to alchemy. This was something the monasteries knew a lot about. It would not occur to Italian monks to prescribe beer but things were different in northern Europe. Throughout the Middle Ages drinking water and even milk of any kind was hazardous because of the generally poor sanitary conditions. Brewing ale, by contrast, involved its own sterilisation processes. Around AD 800 monasteries in Germany and Switzerland discovered that the addition of hops provided even greater benefits for preservation and shelf life, and real beer was born. Monasteries could use the best ingredients, had dedicated and clean utensils and were committed to the best standards of production as a religious duty. They produced different qualities and strengths of beer for different recipients, some for their own use, and others for travellers and the poor. Many became centres of commercial brewing, a tradition that still exists in the modern Trappist communities.

We know less about this system in England where there was a strong resistance to the introduction of hopped beer. Nevertheless, all institutions, even schools, had facilities for brewing their own such beverages which were a normal part of many people's diet and healthier to drink than the water. Locals often paid into a fund to hold a large brewing session for community celebrations. Similarly, Church Ales raised money for the Church or for charitable causes. In many parishes the most important of these was the Whitsun Ale. The seventeenth century antiquarian, John Aubrey, wrote:

> There were no rates for the poor in my grandfather's days but for Kingston St Michael (no small parish) the Church Ale of Whitsuntide did the business. In every parish is (or was) a church-house to which belonged spits, crocks, etc., utensils for dressing provisions. Here the housekeepers met, and were merry and gave their charity. The young people were there too, and had dancing, bowling, shooting at butts, etc., the ancients sitting gravely by, and looking on. All things were civil and without scandal.

Two men were selected every year to be Wardens so that they could collect together money and all the necessary provisions. In some places honorary posts were set up for elected Lords and Ladies of the Ale or Whitsun Kings and Queens. Such Church Ales probably developed further to replace the extended social functions of the monasteries after they were abolished in the sixteenth century.

For much of the medieval period day-to-day drink was provided by local alewives who did not have an unalloyed reputation for quality if we take John Skelton's *Elynour Rummynge* into account:

> For, as ill a place as that,
> The hens run in the mash vat;
> For they go to roost,
> Straight over the ale jug,
> And dung when it comes,
> In the ale tuns.
> Then Eleanor takes the mash bowl, and shakes
> The hens dung away,
> And skims it into a tray
> Where the yeast is,
> With her mangy fists.
> And sometimes she blends

The dung of her hens
And the ale together,
And says, 'Gossip, come hither
This ale shall be thicker,
And flower the more quickly;
For I may tell you,
I learnt it off a Jew,
When I began to brew,
And I have found it true.
Drink now while it is new;
And you can digest,
It will make you look
Younger than you be
Years two or three,
For you may prove it by me.'

Nowadays the six-pointed star is most closely associated with the State of Israel. Are we to interpret John Skelton's reference to Elynour Runnyge having learnt her craft from a Jew as meaning that there was a Jewish involvement in the brewing industry in Elizabethan England? This seems unlikely.

The Israeli hexagram, the Star of David, is not generally regarded as a historical Jewish symbol. The ancient recognised symbols of Judaism were the scroll of the *Torah* and the seven branched candelabrum, the *Menorah*. A survey of more than a thousand Jewish sculptures and ceremonial objects from the Graeco-Roman period produced only four clearly defined six-pointed stars.[3] These may have been mere decoration. The Shield of David, or *Magan Dawid*, was used by medieval Jews as a protective symbol on amulets intended to fend off disease and occasionally appeared on synagogues and in manuscripts but was never mentioned in rabbinical literature. The same six-pointed star was also found in Christian contexts, even on the walls of cathedrals in Germany, and may have been a widely recognised protective device derived from Kabbalistic sources.[4] Jews also used the five-pointed star, sometimes referred to as Solomon's Seal. In 1354 King Charles IV of Bohemia donated a red flag to the Jews of Prague which had a five-pointed and a six-pointed star on it. The Star of David started to be promoted by Zionists in the nineteenth century. Its present identity owes most to its selection by the Nazis as a derogatory sign to single out Jews. The response to this in other countries, particularly America, was to invert the process and claim the star as the main symbol of Zionism and it was taken up by the state of Israel in 1948.[5]

The reference in *Elynour Runnyge* may have had more to do with the virtue of chicken products. It is unlikely that there were many Jews in Elizabethan England. They were expelled from the country by Edward I in 1290 and not formally readmitted until 1655. Jews are recorded as brewers, distillers and tavern owners in Eastern Europe and Russia from the sixteenth century onwards after their arrival in the Pale of Settlement. They leased breweries and taverns from local estates and in parts of Poland and Russia in the seventeenth century up to 30 per cent of the tavern owners were Jewish. In the Russian district of Volhynia in 1602 Jewish brewers were instructed to take down a sign showing that drink was available on the Sabbath. Unfortunately, we are not told what sort of sign it was. It could have been a six-pointed beer star but this would presumably have been the same sign that others in the industry used. The willingness of Jews to take on the production and supply of drink started to backfire later when anti-Semitic sentiments rose to fore. They were accused of exploiting the peasants and forcing them into drunkenness and penury.[6]

For the Seven Stars, it is almost regarded as a commonplace that many early inns, such as the one in Tamerton Foliot, started out as monastic hostels which were later privatised. Precise information about these is difficult to pin down and the destruction of the monasteries during Henry VIII's reign may have led to the loss of much of this. Quite a few village Seven Stars are next to churches and in the case of South Tawton the original church-house is directly opposite. The Seven Stars in Riddings, Derbyshire, was built on top of an earlier St Magdalen's Chapel. Many aspects of medieval brewing and viniculture were intimately bound up with the culture of monasteries, and the symbolism attached to them could have been influenced by the Neoplatonic beliefs in alchemy and astrology that were found there.

If the sign of the Seven Stars had a Christian origin, as many have suggested, then the distribution of the older pubs with that name should show some parallels with the early spread of monastic and church institutions. However, there appears to be little connection. Anglo-Saxon shrines and eleventh century monasteries and abbeys were found across most of the central and lowland areas of England including East Anglia and the eastern seaboard. Celtic monasteries were also present in Scotland from the earliest times at places like Iona in the Western Isles and Portmahomack on the Tain Peninsular. The geographical spread of old Seven Stars is much more restricted than this.

On the left the minsters and monasteries present in England C. 1035 (after Stenton, 1971), and on the right the locations of Anglo-Saxon shrines and places of pilgrimage (after Webb, 2000)

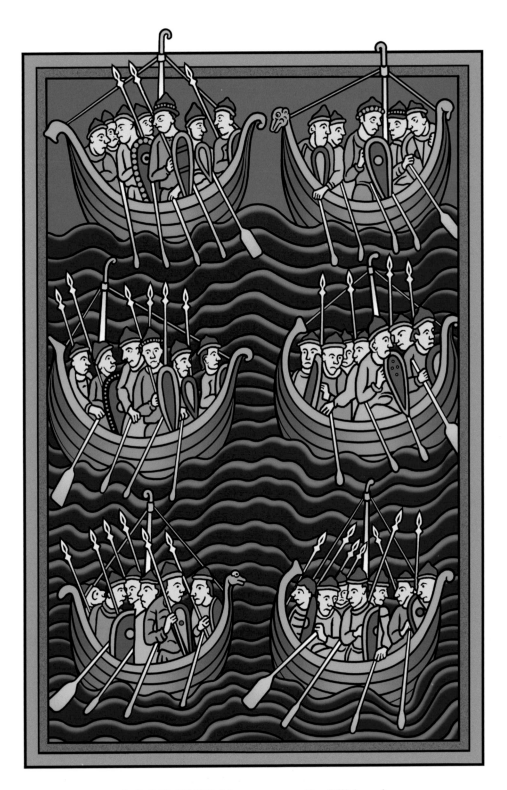

LOOK OUT! Here come the Vikings!

THE ANGLO-SAXONS AND THE DANES

It is easy to get hung up over arguments about the dates that are bandied about for some inns and public houses, or even to be concerned about which is the oldest pub in a particular town, city or even the whole of England. We know that in the Middle Ages alehouses were just that — houses, probably sometimes consisting of little more than a living and sleeping room and a kitchen, where ale was occasionally brewed and where a generic sign was put up for the occasion. The writings of André Simon and Thomas Dekker show that during the Tudor and Jacobean periods any workshop or private house was free to buy a licence from the Crown to sell wine or provide beer as a sideline. Many such outlets, by their very nature, must have been ephemeral. Inns and larger taverns, on the other hand, would have been more distinct and permanent. They would have been strategically placed for obvious commercial reasons which changed little over the centuries until modern railways, motor transport and urban development disrupted the old lines of communication. Some buildings can be dated by precise methods such as the dendrochronology of the oldest timbers they contain. Chance records are available that show a particular inn or tavern was functioning at a particular date, or graffiti survive, such as that in Dawes Green, which offer opinions by satisfied or dissatisfied customers from the past. None of these tell us how long that building or previous ones on the same site had existed before that date, in what condition they were in or what they were originally used for.

Even if you can come up with few certifiable dates, these are isolated pieces of information which do not provide a broad basis for drawing any general conclusions about the history of pubs or the meanings of their signs. However, it is possible to look at this problem from another direction. It is generally clear which pubs are old and which more modern, give or take few centuries. This provides a reasonably reliable sample of old hostelries which can be compared with other kinds of information that may predate some of the pubs themselves.

Twenty-four Seven Stars have been identified as dating from between the fourteenth and seventeenth centuries (Appendix A). The evidence for some of these may debatable but this need not necessarily affect the overall conclusions. Two of these have recently closed and three no longer physically exist but sufficient interesting historical information survives for them to be included. As has already been noted, if you plot these older Seven Stars on a map of mainland Britain they show a very restricted and strange distribution. It does not require sophisticated statistical analysis to prove that this is non-random. They are found across the south of England from Kent to Cornwall and in a narrow strip

The distribution of Seven Stars that existed before the end of the seventeenth century and the English Law Codes as described in the Laws of William the Conqueror

up through the West Midlands into southern Lancashire. There are none in the east of England north of the Thames or in the North, Wales or Scotland.

We noted in previous chapters how some early inns and hostelries may have been involved with the Church and there have been many suggestions by a variety of people over the years that the sign of the Seven Stars had a religious significance. However, as we have seen, the distribution of abbeys, monasteries and the shrines of saints in medieval England show no relationship with the older Seven Stars. This is as near as we can get to proving that the Seven Stars sign had nothing to do with the Christian religion and its early involvements with hospitality or brewing. However, more remarkably, the distribution of these old Seven Stars is an almost exact reflection of the local government structure of England during the late Saxon period following the Viking incursions of the ninth century and up to and beyond the Norman invasion of 1066.

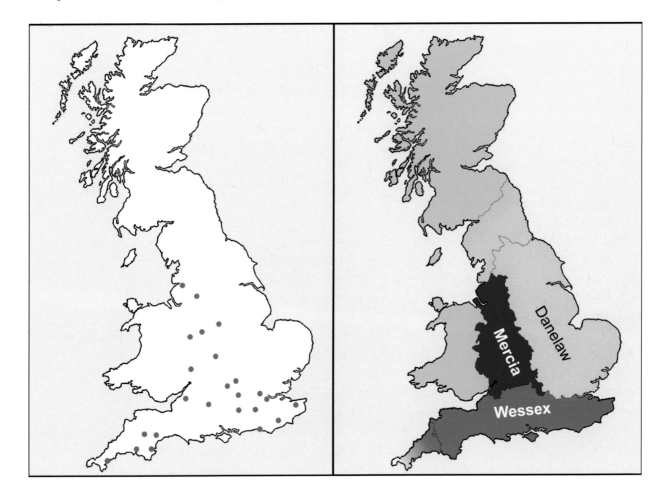

Roman control of England from around AD 40 to 400 created a sophisticated network of urban centres and road networks over most of the country. The last Roman garrisons were withdrawn by Emperor Constantine III in 407 to deal with problems on the continental mainland. Native Britons then seem to have fought among themselves to set up local fiefdoms but these were immediately subject to attack by invading Germanic tribes from the northern Rhineland and Denmark. Some of these may have been invited in as mercenaries but their relatives eventually formed a new Teutonic elite that took over most of England. By the end of the seventh century the country had been divided into three main tribal groupings. The West Saxons from northern Germany eventually ruled most of the south of England, now called Wessex, excluding Cornwall. The Angles from further to the north ruled what is now East Anglia as well as much of the eastern seaboard. The largest central area covering all the Midlands and beyond was the separate kingdom of Mercia ruled by other families of Anglian descent. This was the most powerful for much of the period but, at one time or another, the ruler of any one might claim to be the King of all of England.

The fabric of the Roman Empire gradually crumbled during this period and was replaced by a more rural society centred on villages. By middle Saxon times much of England had been divided into the shires that we now recognise as counties, each run by an ealdorman. In principle, each shire was centred on a defendable town with its own court. This system may have been started by Alfred the Great. The basic farming and taxation unit was a 'hide' and a hundred hides was a 'hundred' with its own local court, a 'moot'. With variations, this system covered most of the country. Some parts of the Roman infrastructure must have survived, such as well used roads, inns and taverns, although how conscious the people living at the time were of the origins of these is debatable. When parts of the Roman road between London and Silchester re-emerged in the later Middle Ages people were so amazed at its construction and straightness that they thought it must be of supernatural origin and called it the Devil's Highway.

In the ninth century the Angles and Saxons themselves were subject to new invasions by Danes and Norsemen from across the North Sea. 'Heathen men' first appeared on the Isle of Sheppey in 835. By 879 the Danes had become established in all the Anglo-Saxon kingdoms except Wessex. Their intention was to take over the whole of England but it was Alfred the Great and his cakes that saved the day. After a protracted war in 886 the Danes were accepted as the established rulers of all the east of England north of the Thames and as far as the southern half of Watling Street to the west.

The treaty that was signed between Alfred and the Danish leader Guthrum effectively established a form of apartheid which not only defined their respective territories but also forbade anybody crossing the boundary unless they had special permission to trade.

Nominally, Alfred remained the King of England but according to the Anglo-Saxon Chronicle he was only king of those who were free to offer him their allegiance. The area he did not control became known as the Danelaw where Scandinavian laws and customs held sway. Later English kings, such as Edgar, recognised the status quo and expected the Danes to keep the peace provided they were allowed to hang on to their own traditions:

> moreover it is my will that among the Danes such good laws shall be valid
> as they best appoint

During the next 130 years there were repeated Danish invasions. In most cases the invaders were bought off and persuaded to stay where they were by paying them large sums of money that had been raised by taxing the English. This was the Danegeld which formed the model for future taxation by the Crown. Between 991 and 1014 it is estimated that over 150,000 lbs of silver were handed to the Danes to keep them quiet.

Æthelred (the longest serving Saxon king despite his later reputation) occasionally saw fit to make special laws for the Danelaw through his Archbishop, Wulfstan, when he thought it necessary. He also thought that he could solve the Danish problem by massacring all of those he could get his hands on during St Brice's Day in 1012. In retaliation, the largest Danish invasion then began under Swein Forkbeard. Eventually Swein's son, Cnut, and Æthelred's successor, Edmund Ironside, fought each other to a standstill and agreed that they could share the English crown and that it would pass to the survivor. Edmund then mysteriously died in London only a month later and Cnut (known more often by his English name Canute) became King of England in 1016.[1]

As King of England, Denmark and Norway, Cnut was in position to control all further Viking activity. Despite rapidly killing off any Anglo-Saxon royalty who he thought might threaten his rule, he retained much of the administrative structure that had been inherited from them. He divided England up into four groups of shires, Wessex, Mercia, East Anglia and Northumbria, with an earl in charge of each. The Earls of Wessex and Mercia were in fact from Anglo-Saxon families, thus maintaining the cultural distinctions that had been established over a hundred years before.

Much of Cnut's legacy was carried on by the next invader, William the Conqueror, in 1066. The Normans are known for centralising power under the king and introducing the feudal system. However, when it came to local government they continued the late Anglo-Saxon and Danish divisions and the law codes that seem to have gone with them, partly because they worked and partly to emphasise continuity and the legitimacy of their claim to England.

The legal landscape of England after the Danish invasions was first recorded under

Cnut and survived into a twelfth century document, the *Laws of William the Conqueror*.[2] It provides a clear breakdown of how the English shires were split up (Appendix B). The West-Saxon area (generally abbreviated to Wessex) covered the whole of the south of England from Kent to Devon. The Mercian area was most restricted, stretching from Oxfordshire to the Welsh border and up to Cheshire. Modern Lancashire south of the Ribble was part of Cheshire. The land north of this had been under Norse control and was treated as part of Yorkshire until the Duchy and Palatinate were established in the fourteenth century. The Danelaw itself was divided into four separate regions: East Anglia; the south-east Midlands; the Five Boroughs of Lincoln, Nottingham, Derby, Leicester and Stamford; and Northumbria.

The differences between the West Saxon and Mercian codes would have been quite minor, so the main division was between the Danes in the east and the Anglo-Saxons in the south and west. Little is known of the Danish laws because they were probably originally orally transmitted by a few 'speakers' who were called in by the aristocracy when required. Some of the Anglo-Saxon administrative units were maintained but given Scandinavian names. The exact boundaries of all these areas were probably much more fluid than the above descriptions indicate and were unlikely to have corresponded precisely to the modern counties. Cornwall presented an anomalous position as a bastion of Celtic Britons in England. Cornish revolts were defeated by the Saxons in 838 and around 930 when the River Tamar was established as an official boundary to the county. Therefore throughout the Anglo-Saxon period the Cornish probably still had their own customs and laws which were not subject to those of Wessex. However, after the Norman Conquest there was little to stop Englishness invading the county. Wales and Scotland were entirely separate under native Celtic and Norse rule.

Like the Angles and Saxons, the Danes were Christianised shortly after they settled in the east of England. The Danish king Cnut (King of England from 1016-1035) was influenced by Anglo-Saxon churchmen and may have been a Christian before he arrived in 1016. He was keen to emphasise his legitimacy as a modern Christian monarch by visiting Rome and supporting centres of pilgrimage such as the Abbey of Bury St Edmunds. Ironically, this was the shrine of a Anglian king martyred by the invading Danes in 869 (some think that St Edmund should be the real patron saint of England rather than that largely mythical foreigner St George). Therefore there is no reason to believe that any of the differences between the Danelaw and the Anglo-Saxon regions came from divergence in the fundamentals of religion. The Danish laws must have been based on social traditions and political organisations that came from northern Europe, emphasising the local distribution of power among war bands and ship's companies, and more strongly Scandinavian than the Germanic ancestry of the Angles and Saxons.

*The remains
of the transept
and the nave
of the Abbey of
St Edmund in
Bury*

At home nobody told the Vikings what to do. They had to be persuaded to band together by promises of riches or fame in Valhalla. It would perhaps be presumptuous to suggest that England was a more civilised country than Denmark in the ninth century but the Vikings were certainly regarded as coming from a barbarian and more violent culture, even though the Anglo-Saxons themselves were no angels, contrary to the earlier opinions of Pope Gregory.[3] For instance, we are told stories of the Vikings carrying out the 'blood eagle' sacrifices to Wodin of the Kings of Northumbria and East Anglia where their lungs were torn out through their ribcages and spread over their backs like wings. Some of this may have been propaganda. The alternative version is that St Edmund was tied to a tree and shot full of arrows before being beheaded.

The shock of the Danish invasions led Alfred the Great to believe that they were a punishment from the Almighty for the sinfulness and ignorance of the English. He tried to alter this by promoting classical culture. Many Latin texts, 'the books most necessary for all men to know', were translated into English during his reign, some by the king himself. Anybody who was not born a serf was sent to school and taught to read. In many ways the original Anglo-Saxons must also have been the direct inheritors of what was left of Roman culture from the fourth and fifth centuries, some of which would have persisted among the native Britons that they governed. Christianity carried on in the west in what was later known as the Celtic Church. This eventually came into conflict with later Catholicism when the heathen Saxons were converted by missions sent directly from Rome by Pope Gregory the Great in the sixth century. We should therefore look for more Mediterranean influences on the cultures of Wessex and Mercia than in the Danelaw.

Although elites of all stripes were committed to the luxury of imported wines, the Danes did not come from a wine-drinking culture and would have had their own recipes for brewed liquors as well as the ones they found in the east of England. They presumably also had places for drinking them that might not have been the same as those of the natives. We know something about this because of a connection between drinking and violence.

Norman followers of French chivalry were upset at the brutality they found in Anglo-Scandinavian politics. Shortly after he came to the throne Cnut had rounded up and murdered every Anglo-Saxon he could lay his hands on who might have any claim to the monarchy. Æthelred tried to solve the Danish problem through genocide, only leading to revenge attacks by the Danes. One of the fundamentals in law that was common to all at this time was the *wergild*, a fine that people had to pay if they had killed somebody. This was set at different levels depending upon the status of the victim and which code the fight or crime was committed under. Violent death was accepted as part of the culture but it was considered politically desirable to prevent such events from escalating into family or tribal blood feuds. It contributed more to the peace if blood money was paid.

During the reign of Æthelred a new set of laws was drawn by the Archbishop of York, Wulfstan, which was directed specifically at the Danelaw, particularly the Five Boroughs. This has become known as the *Wantage Code* after the town on the borders of Berkshire and Oxfordshire where it was signed by the King in 997. It is most remembered for referring to a jury of twelve thegns who were sworn-in for conducting cases. This concept of a sworn jury, which is now the basis of much jurisprudence, seems to have been a Scandinavian custom which was previously unknown in England.

Within the Code there is a passage which sets out fines for breaches of the peace in assemblies. These were centred on the borough, the wapentake and the alehouse. The boroughs were the highest civil administrative unit. Wapentake (the equivalent of a Saxon 'hundred') was a Scandinavian term which referred to a more local assembly of armed men who set aside their swords and axes during the debate and then flourished them at the end to acknowledge a decision. For the last, the eminent scholar of the Anglo-Saxon period, Sir Frank Stenton, is said to have expressed amazement that the king should concern himself with what went on in alehouses around Lincoln. He concluded from the scale of the fines that they were actually more than mere alehouses but an important part of the Danish local government system where rules and disputes were argued out over a few drinks, the equivalent of the classical system of *in vino veritas* but more *in cervisia veritas*.[4]

> And the peace which is given in an alehouse, it is to be atoned for,
> if a man is killed, with 6 halfmarks, and if no one is killed, with 12 ores.[5]

These laws must have been introduced because the assemblies frequently degenerated to a level where they were sorted out 'after the Viking manner'. Violence in eastern England was something that concerned the monarchy for the next few hundred years. During the reign of Edward I there is a case in the Lincoln Rolls where a Roger Halpeny from Westwood on the Island was, 'by force of arms and against the peace', assaulted and taken to an alehouse (*taberna cervisaria*) where he was forced to drink his own blood mixed with ale under threat of death.[6] In Bury St Edmunds violence between the Abbey and the townsfolk was a part of everyday life. In 1327 the locals tried to burn the Abbey and during the Peasant's Revolt of 1381 they beheaded the Prior and several monks.

We are entitled to conclude from the evidence that there were fundamental differences between the drinking cultures of the surviving old Anglo-Saxon states and those of the Danelaw. It is quite clear that the old Seven Stars are nearly all within the West Saxon and Mercian areas. The only exceptions are very close by. There is one in Cornwall (Falmouth) and another in Derby (itself of somewhat dubious attribution both as regards name and date). The Seven Stars at Dinton in Buckinghamshire was technically in the Danelaw. However, it is near the southern boundary with Oxfordshire and surveying and boundary recording techniques may have been fairly fluid in the distant past. One Seven Stars survives in London, a city which originally belonged to the East Saxons and was regained for Wessex by Alfred the Great in 886.

How does this distribution apply to modern pubs and hotels with the Seven Stars name? Identifying all of these is not easy given the errors and omissions in most printed directories and the prevalence of out of date web pages. The best attempt is listed in Appendix C which shows all the eighty-one Seven Stars that were probably open in the year 2000. More than three quarters (62 or 77 per cent) are still in the eleventh century Saxon and Mercian areas. This rises to 68 or 84 per cent if you include Cornwall. As with the old establishments, it does not require the use of formal statistical tests to indicate a significant geographical relationship. Severe statisticians will tell you that correlation is not the same as causation, but it is difficult to avoid the suggestion that the sign of the Seven Stars is a remnant of Romanised Anglo-Saxon culture surviving from at least the ninth or tenth centuries AD.

THE CELESTIAL GRAPES

The true meaning of a symbol can be properly understood only in the context of its time. As a society changes the symbol may persist but the meaning alters. Inns called the Seven Stars have certainly been around for the last 700 years. The buildings have been replaced but in many cases the name seems to have lived on. However, the distribution of the oldest pubs with that name can be linked to the time of the Anglo-Saxons before the Danish invasions of the ninth century AD, a span of years that is nearly twice as long. How are we to interpret this fact?

One explanation is that there have been hostelries with that kind of sign outside in particular places going back to middle Anglo-Saxon, possibly even late Roman times. This is not impossible but coming up with firm evidence for the idea probably is. It could even be questioned whether some of the places involved were actually inhabited at the time. On the other hand, it has been pointed out that nearly all the villages present in modern England were already recorded in the Domesday Book and some of the local government structures that are first recorded under the Anglo-Saxons may have derived from earlier Celtic and Iron Age practices.

It is difficult to avoid the suggestion that the precise distribution pattern of the early Seven Stars is derived from the West Saxon and Mercian legal codes. Possibly this was no more than a rule that active hostelries had to have some sort of sign outside so that the local authorities could identify them and keep control over what was going on in towns and villages. These signs may have been influenced by popular classical learning. For instance, there is a suggestion that pub names based on Aesop's Fables, such as the Fox and Grapes, may also have been restricted to the same areas.[1] Unfortunately the sample size is too small to be sure of this. By contrast, after the ninth century in the Scandinavian dominated areas of the Danelaw, alehouses may have been seen primarily as community centres where drink was available as an adjunct to official activities which required no special sign to advertise their presence because the buildings involved were themselves already part of the legal structure.

We know that in England in the later Middle Ages there were times when legally specified signs such as ale-stakes were required. We have no evidence as to whether this was the case during the Anglo-Saxon period. The signs that were used are likely to have been based on an old tradition of symbolism which carried on up until the Restoration period and which people naturally fell back on when they wanted to put up a sign for a particular kind of drink or accommodation. This tradition, probably with a Graeco-Roman background and older links to the ancient Middle East, had become established in the Anglo-Saxon kingdoms under some sort of legal sanction. It was foreign to the Scandinavian invaders of the ninth and tenth centuries who, in the interests of peace, were allowed to carry on their own laws and customs. They seem to have had different ideas about the designation and even the function and ownership of drinking establishments. As a result, the sign of the Seven Stars persisted in the south and west of England, but was totally extinguished in the east and north. Nothing else can explain the clear cut geographical split in the early distribution of the sign between the Anglo-Saxon remnants of England and the Danelaw. Even though England nominally became a unified Kingdom after the time of Cnut, such cultural distinctions seem to have carried on well past the Norman invasion and, in this particular instance, only started breaking down from the eighteenth century onwards. From that time on the name of the Seven Stars survived out of custom or inertia. It may also have started to mean different things to different people which they wished to express through a pub sign.

There is little doubt that this tradition was related to the star formation which we recognise by its Greek name of the Pleiades. The idea that this asterism is composed of seven stars, which bears little relation to physical reality, goes back to the earliest records that we have of European and Middle Eastern astronomy and must itself have been based on an older tradition of religious symbolism that was probably related to moon worship. There are two ways in which star formations can insinuate their ways into minds attuned to symbolism: by their seasonal appearance; and by their form.

Even if they did not study the sky themselves, those with access to the classical literature should have been quite aware of the seasonal significance of the Pleiades. However, the Venerable Bede, writing around AD 725 in *On the Nature of Things* said:

> Pleiades are hight the seven stars which in harvest go up, and during all
> winter shine going from east westward. During the summer they go at
> night time under the earth and by day stay above it.

For somebody who is supposed to have been well schooled in astronomy and one of the architects of the calculation of the date for Easter, this seems to be a rather superficial description. As we saw earlier, the Roman month of May gets its name from the rising of the Pleiades. Perhaps this was part of a wider Anglo-Saxon opinion that the Pleiades were primarily associated with the dates of harvest.

While to the casual observer the Pleiades seem like a smudge in the sky, to many stargazers in the ancient world they evoked particular patterns and images. One of the best established of these is that they were a flock of doves. Several Greek poets chose to connect them with the Greek for dove or pigeon, *peleia*, and called the resulting flock the Peleiades. A fragment from Simonides dating to the early fifth century BC says:

> Hermes, lord of the games, grants the prayer,
> He the child of mountain Maya of the black-eyes. Atlas bred her,
> The fairest in beauty of his seven dear dark-haired daughters,
> Who are called Doves of the skies.[2]

The main motivation for this was their appearance as these birds in various stories from Greek mythology. The most well-known of these concerns the constellation of the giant headless hunter Orion who, after consuming the local vintage, boasted that he would rid the whole world of its animals. The earth Goddess was so shocked by this that she sent a giant scorpion to kill him and the two still chase each other round the sky. While travelling through Boeotia (the centre of the cult of Dionysos) Orion was so enamoured of the daughters of Pleione that he chased them around for seven years before Zeus saved them and placed them in the sky as doves.

Another story concerning the sisters is that they were doves to begin with and carried ambrosia to the infant Zeus before becoming stars. Other references to the Pleiades being doves come from late scholastic commentators on the Greek poets. There are sufficient allusions to the Pleiades being such birds in Greek poetry and mythology that all listeners must have known such stories. They presumably did not need to be spelled out and must have had some earlier independent existence which was amplified by later poets and mythographers.

The eminent Scottish zoologist Sir D'Arcy Wentworth Thompson, during the time he had to spare from inventing Structural Zoology and Marine Biology, published a book in 1895 (reprinted in 1936) called *A Glossary of Greek Birds* in which he catalogued the names of all the birds he could find in ancient Greek literature. He discussed the various words used for doves and pigeons by the Greeks. The principal ones are *peleia*, *peristera* and *oinas*. While these were used as general words for pigeon or dove they generally referred more specifically to the Rock Dove (*Columba livia*) and its domesticated variety the Domestic Pigeon (more exact words were used for other birds such as the Turtle Dove, *trygon*). Thompson suggests *oinas* may have been a foreign bird name introduced to Greece from the east and sometimes referred to the Stock Dove (*Columba oenas*). Both this and the Rock Dove have distinctive iridescent green and purple neck and breast feathers. *Oinas* is, of course, also the more common ancient Greek word for vine or vinous, and *oinos* meant wine, leading to the connection between the colour of some of the bird's feathers and the colour of red grapes and wine. The Stock Dove appeared in Greece on migration at the time of the grape harvest. Thompson also refers to coins from the Cretan colony of Mallos near Tarsus in Asia Minor which showed a dove with a bunch of grapes for its breast.[3]

Another mythological connection between doves and wine is found in the story of the daughters of Anius, King of Delos. These were called the *Oinotrophoi* or the Wine Growers. They could magically turn whatever they touched into staple food crops, Elais for Olive (*elaia*), Spermo for Seed (*sperma*) and Oeno for Wine (*oinos*). These were an obvious catch for anybody who wanted to fill their larders:

> King Anius shook his head, whereon he ware a mitre bright,
> And answered thus: O noble prince, in faith thou guessest right.
> Of children five a father then thou diddest me behold,
> Who now (with such inconstancy are mortal matters rolled)
> Am in a manner childless quite. For what avails my son
> Who in the Isle of Anderland a great way hence doth wone?
> Which country takes his name of him. And in the selfsaid place,
> Instead of father, like a king he holds the royal mace.
> Apollo gave his lot to him; and Bacchus, for to show
> His love, a greater gift upon his sisters did bestow
> Than could be wished or credited. For whatsoever they
> Did touch was turned into corn and wine and oil straightway.
> And so there was rich use in them. As soon as that the fame
> Hereof to Agamemnon's ears, the scourge of Trojans, came,
> Lest you might taste your storms alone and we not feel the same
> In part, an host he hither sent and, whether I would or no,
> Did take them from me, forcing them among the Greeks to go
> To feed the Greekish army with their heavenly gift. But they
> Escapèd whither they could by flight. A couple took their way
> To Isle Euobea; t'other two to Anderland did fly,
> Their brother's realm. An host of men pursued them by and by
> And threatened war unless they were delivered. Force of fear,
> Subduing nature, did constrain the brother (men must bear
> With fearfulness) to render up his sisters to their foe.
> For neither was Aeneas there nor valiant Hector (who
> Did make your war last ten years long) the country to defend.
> Now when they like prisoners have been fettered, in the end
> They, casting up their hands (which yet were free) to heaven did cry

To Bacchus for to succour them; who helped them by and by —
At leastwise if it may be termed a help in wondrous wise
To alter folk. For never could I learn ne can surmise
The manner how they lost their shape. The thing itself is known.
With feathered wings as white as snow they quite away are flown,
Transformed into dovehouse doves, thy wise Dame Venus' birds.
Ovid's Metamorphoses translated by Arthur Golding (1567).

The association between the dove and wine was established early on in Christian symbolism and the connection with the Pleiades may never have been lost. Isidore, who lived from AD 570 to 636, was an archbishop of Seville who wrote widely on classical and theological subjects. He produced an encyclopaedia in twenty volumes called the *Etymologies*, in one of which he derived the meanings of Greek and Latin words from a variety of ancient sources and, to some extent, his own imagination. He associated the Pleiades with the Latin word *Butrum*, derived from the Greek *botrus* meaning a 'bunch of grapes' based on a reference from the Younger Theon who was an Alexandrian mathematician and astronomer of the fourth century AD.[4] Nowadays many of Isidore's derivations are regarded with suspicion, but he was one of the most widely read authors throughout Europe for the next 800 years and nearly a thousand medieval manuscripts of the *Etymologies* still survive. Therefore, most educated people would have been familiar with it and the ideas it contained.

However, this visual association which saw the Pleiades as a bunch of grapes may go back much further. I have argued elsewhere, in *Foxes from the Gods*, that there were two parallel traditions in the Greek world which derived from the visualisation of animal constellations in the night sky. These were associated with the constellation which we now chose to call Cetus, the Whale. If you view this constellation as pointing east, there is a parallelogram of stars at its front end which looks like a head with two projections from it. These can be seen as the beard and horns of a billy goat or the snout and ears of a fox. The whole constellation in the western sky during the autumn appears like one of these animals standing on its hind legs with its head just underneath the Pleiades.[5]

The goat interpretation can be seen as a fundamental part of the Dionysian and Bacchic world view. Sacrifice of a billy goat was one of the hallmarks of Dionysian worship and was also performed in vineyards to propitiate the vintage throughout the Mediterranean classical period. We have records of this from early Greek references by the Greek poet Leonidas of Tarentum in the third century BC up until the verse of the Roman poet Martial in the first century AD.[6] The billy goat was first castrated and then had its throat cut unceremoniously (as compared with the formal care taken when sacrificing bulls

One face of a seal from the Temple Repository at Knossos, Crete, last half of the second millennium BC

and rams). The story surrounding this act was always that the goat was being punished for eating grapes. The most consistent explanation of this cult is that it was a reaction to what was being seen in the stars where the goat was interpreted as attacking the celestial grapes (the Pleiades) and that it was hoped the sacrifice would please Dionysos in the heavenly realm and bring his blessing on the wine harvest. This aspect of Greek religion probably came up through the islands from Crete. It may be reflected in the image on a seal from the Late Palace Period at Knossos of the second millennium BC which shows a billy goat next to seven dots.[7] In his book *On Agriculture* from BC 35, the Roman writer Marcus Terentius Varro says that the offspring of the goat Capricorn was placed in the sky outside the zodiac next to the bull Taurus but does not provide any more information on the subject.[8] This sort of pagan Bacchic imagery was probably widely known about throughout Europe in the past. For instance, during the late Middle Ages in Germany the bulbous glass bottle used in monasteries to hold wine was known as a *Bocksbeutel* or 'goat's scrotum'.

The fox interpretation is exemplified by one of Aesop's *Fables*, the well-know one of the Fox and the Grapes. We know that these fables came to Greece from the Near East via Asia Minor because we are told so by an early versifier of the fables called Babrius. He says in the introduction to the second part of his work that they were invented by the ancient Syrians.[9] Babrius was a tutor to the son of King Alexander of Cilicia during the second century AD. Living near what is now the border between Turkey and Syria, he was in a good position to know what he was talking about. The form of the fable can be closely linked to the Wisdom Literature of ancient Mesopotamia. For instance, it is widely recognised that the fable of the Eagle and the Fox is based on the Assyrian myth of the *Legend of Etana*.[10] The earlier Sumerian Wisdom Literature from the third millennium BC contains hundreds of Proverbs. Thirty-seven of these refer to the fox in some way and several of these can be easily interpreted as referring to this fox constellation in the sky.[11] Images of the Fox and the Grapes appear on Greek vases and engraved gems from the fifth century BC. The same Fox and Grapes can also be seen on a stamp seal from the late Persian Sassanian period of the third century AD. The last cataloguer of these seals in the collection of the British Museum was quite happy with the suggestion that the images on them were conventional pictures of star maps and were a form of astral symbolism.[12]

Left:
an engraved
Greek gem from
the fifth century
BC showing the
Fox and Grapes.
Right:
a similar image
from a Persian
seal of the third
century AD

This would not be of much relevance if the Anglo-Saxons were abstemious or teetotal, but the evidence suggests the opposite. They had plenty of words for drink of all kinds. The principal kinds were *beor, meodu, ealu* and *win*. Contrary to the way in which it has often been translated in the past, *beor* was probably cider made from apples or pears.[13] *Meodu* was mead made from honey, *ealu* was ale and *win*, wine. They also had words for all the three parts of the hospitality industry that we know from later years. There was the alehouse — *ealahus* or *ealuhus*; the tavern — *winhus* or *winærn*; and the inn – *cumenhus*. Riotous drinking at weddings, funerals and other social events is well attested in the literature throughout the period.

There are occasional references to alehouses in early legislation. King Æthelbert of Kent tried to restrict the number in 616 as did Ine of Wessex in 688. Æthelbert, suggesting the risks that came with a regional peripatetic monarchy, was severe on any crimes committed while the king was feasting and drinking in somebody else's household. The fullest known legislation is from the reign of King Edgar (around 960). He attempted to restrict the number of alehouses to one per village and brought in rules for putting pegs in drinking horns and cups. When a communal cup was passed round you were only allowed to drink the measure between successive pegs. Penalties were laid down for infractions but how the law was meant to be administered is anybody's guess. This may have been to replace a custom where amounts of drink for different people in a company were measured by sticking a finger in the cup down to the depth of successive joints.

Despite apparently having a name for an inn, the role of such institutions in society during this period is obscure. Early Anglo-Saxon culture had a tradition of hospitality in one's own house for strangers which may have reduced the need for commercial inns. This could be qualified. In the Laws of Ine it was decreed that no household was obliged to offer hospitality if they did not want to. On the other hand, the Laws of Æthelred had a clause saying that people 'should not vex and oppress strangers and men come from afar'. One piece of evidence that has been put forward for the existence of inns is that in a number of Latin law codes, particularly that of Edward the Confessor, it was said that anybody who was a guest in somebody's house for more than three nights should be treated as the responsibility of the householder if they had committed a crime.[14]

> But if he has lodged on the third night, and he commits an offence against
> anyone, let him by right be treated as a member of the family, for the
> English say: *þa nihte gist, þridde niht ogene heþen*.

The meaning of this is obscure but is something like: 'Two nights a guest, the third night his own household servant'. This sounds less like behaviour at an ordinary inn and more like a tradition governing how long somebody was regarded as a guest before they could be ordered about by their host. In addition, after the Anglo-Saxons were converted to Christianity there were a large number of monastic hostels which catered for travellers of all kinds. The name for these was a *gesthus*. Another term, related to *cumenhus*, was *cumenabur* which may have described a charitable hospice for travellers. The hospital of St. Peter at York was founded for this purpose by King Æthelstan in 937. Such hospices were a normal part of the medieval scene. St. Katherine's Hospital in Ledbury was founded by Hugh Foliot, Bishop of Hereford, for 'Wayfarers and the Poor' in 1232. On the other hand, contemporary Welsh Laws had provision for lodging houses. No charge could be incurred for the loss of knives, swords or trousers! [15]

The wine-drinking practices of the clergy were frequently a matter of concern. Archbishop Wulfstan, who seems to have been never happier than when making up rules for other people, decreed under Æthelred that priests should not drink in public whereas under Cnut he seems to suggest that they just should not drink in taverns very often and certainly should not get drunk:

> *ne drincan æt wynhuse, ne druncengeorn beon,* becomes
> *ne drincan æt winhusum ealles to gelome, ne to druncangeorn wurðan.*

Anglo-Saxon monasteries of the seventh and eighth centuries seem to have been as much

St Katherine's Hospital, Ledbury

aristocratic clubs as religious institutions, where surplus members of ruling families went for a comfortable life or at least to escape the militaristic environment and reduced life chances of their more active relatives. Not drinking was regarded as an affront to the community. Real saints went off to live under rocks as hermits. A surviving seventh century tract by disciples of the Archbishop of Canterbury called *Theodore's Penitential* gives rules about overindulgence. Any ordained person who was customarily drunk should be dismissed. A presbyter or deacon who vomits should do forty days penance, a monk thirty days, a lay worker fifteen days and a layman seven days. On the other hand, if somebody vomited as a result of infirmity or from gladness at Christmas, Easter or on Saint's Days and had imbibed no more than was commanded by their seniors, they committed no offence.

A monk at the abbey of Ramsey, Byrthferth, wrote an account of a service to commemorate the founder in 991 after which there was a big party. He says: 'I was given all sorts of wine and mead to drink in great abundance'. After a ceremony to celebrate the laying of the foundations of a church in Abingdon by King Eadred of Wessex, the

Finds of imported Mediterranean pottery in mainland Britain from the fifth and sixth centuries (after Cunliffe, 2013)

local abbot invited everybody to a nearby hall, the doors were locked and mead flowed all night (some said miraculously) so that many of the congregation passed out. In a later case in 1016, Eadnoth, the Bishop of Dorchester, was killed in the Battle of Assandun. Monks were carrying the body back to his home abbey of Ramsey and stopped overnight in Ely. There one of the Holy Fathers, Æfgar, got them drunk and stole the body of the bishop so that it could become a valuable relic at Ely instead of Ramsey.[16] The Danes were equally keen on their drink. When they first invaded London everybody promptly got drunk on all the imported wine that they could find. King Harthacnut is said 'to have died as he stood at his drink' during a wedding feast in 1041.

That wine continued to be imported from the Mediterranean into England during the fifth and sixth centuries is indicated by the occurrence of distinctive pottery remains from Turkey, Egypt and North Africa which are most heavily concentrated in the West Country. After the sixth century the Mediterranean trade started to dry up but was replaced by wares from western France. While many goods might have been contained in these pots, it is suggested that one of the main drivers of the trade was wine for the remaining Celtic monasteries. A few fragments have been found as far north as Iona.[17]

Before the Romans took over Western Europe much of the trade to England came along the Atlantic seaboard. Roman rule opened up the cross-Channel routes as is shown by the widespread recoveries of wine amphorae of the second century AD over most of England, with some concentrations around the Southampton and Thames areas.[18] After the withdrawal of Roman power there were periods when the North Sea must have been subject to the ravages of Germanic and later Scandinavian pirates so that local traders from the west would have found it safer to bring in goods from western France and Brittany. Later, they may also have benefited from the new sea-going ship building techniques pioneered by the Vikings.

During politically stable periods the Channel routes predominated. Judging by the letters between the Emperor Charlemagne and Offa, the King of Mercia, around 785 much of the commercial and pilgrim traffic of England went through northern France. In the later Saxon period and after the Norman Conquest, the port of Rouen near the mouth of the Seine had a virtual monopoly on the export of French wines to England. After this time trade with the Iberian Peninsula opened up, which also included much pilgrim traffic. During the fourteenth and fifteenth centuries licences were granted by the local bishops to Cornish mariners to carry pilgrims to Santiago de Compostela, Rome and even Jerusalem. There was no single pilgrim's route. Boats are known to have left from Falmouth, Fowey, Landulph, St Michael's Mount, Penzance and Saltash. Bristol and Plymouth were also used for the fortnight long journey to Spain. As wars with France increased in the Middle Ages and later, these routes became more important for trade and Portugal developed as a significant source for wines.

From the ninth to the thirteenth centuries the climate of England was relatively mild and planting vineyards was a practical proposition. Even in the eighth century the Venerable Bede said that wine was grown in some places. In Old English the month of October was sometimes called *wyn monað* because it was the time that grapes were harvested. To begin with this was an enterprise that was largely restricted to monasteries but it must later have been put on a more commercial basis where vineyards could be profitable. Writing in the early twelfth century, William of Malmesbury gives us a description of Gloucestershire:

> You may behold the paths and public roads fenced with apple trees, which are not planted by the hand of man but grow spontaneously. This district, too, exhibits a greater number of vineyards than any other county in England, yielding abundant crops and of superior quality; nor are the wines made here by any means harsh or ungrateful to the palate, for, in point of sweetness, they may almost bear comparison with the growths of France.

Place names with Old English roots that seem to be based on references to vineyards can be found in Devon, Dorset, Gloucestershire, Oxfordshire, Essex, Worcestershire and Cheshire.[19] André Simon suggested that the land around Ledbury must have been particularly suitable for growing vines during the thirteenth century. Much of this would have been on Church land but both abbey and royal account books show that the surplus production was sold off to raise money.[20]

Overleaf:
The Seven Stars,
Dartmouth

CONCLUSIONS

The main conclusion that we can come to is that, from ancient tradition, the Pleiades were seen as a bunch of grapes in the sky and that this imagery was transferred to using the Seven Stars as a sign for wine which was current during late Anglo-Saxon times. Unfortunately, no direct record of such behaviour survives and we are left to rely on indirect lines of evidence for our argument.

The geographical evidence suggests that the sign was used generically during Anglo-Saxon times and was a part of the legal codes that then applied. Since the imagery involved can be easily traced to Mediterranean and Middle Eastern precedents, it may be much older. This does not necessarily mean that there was a building on one site with one sign for the next 1,200 years. Once the tradition for using the Seven Stars had developed, it could be used in any relevant circumstances, however old the actual hostelry that was involved. It only seems to have been in the eighteenth century that the tradition was broken and many people no longer knew what it meant. By then others, such as the Freemasons, may have seen new possibilities in the sign which helped its survival. Even so, modern pubs called the Seven Stars are still mainly found in the areas that they were exclusive to around the time of the Norman Conquest. Who knows at what stage law becomes custom and custom becomes tradition?

Even before the Danes arrived, the sign may always have been used more frequently in the south and west of England. These were the areas where vineyards were commoner due to the advantages of climate. They were also more open to trade from France and the Mediterranean, the main sources of imported wine. In the early Anglo-Saxon period, inns as we know them were probably rare, their position in the community being taken over by private hospitality, monastic hostels and charitable hospitals. On the other hand, it is quite clear that there were alehouses and taverns. These would not have had names as we recognise them today. Some of the signs that they showed to advertise their wares could have been taken over to identify specific buildings during the later Middle Ages but there would have been a need for generic signs advertising wine or beer up until Tudor and Jacobean times. We only know about red lattices as adverts for beer because one source, Thomas Dekker, happened to mention it in passing so there may well have been other signs that escaped active pamphleteers of the time. Wine sellers would have attracted a better cast of customer and therefore been less exposed to criticism.

Much of the wine drunk in England came through ports on the south and south-west coasts. After London, Bristol was the most important port for the import of wine from France and Spain up until the eighteenth century, accounting for about a quarter of all shipments. Bridgewater, Minehead, St. Ives, Plymouth, Dartmouth, Exeter, Weymouth, Poole, Southampton, Chichester, Rye, Romney and Dover all feature in the import records.[1] Even during periods of war with France and Spain, privateers unloaded the cargos from foreign merchantmen that they had commandeered. You also have to add to this the prevalence of smuggling which may have accounted for up to half the imports in some periods, much of it through small ports and coves in the south-west.

Tokens issued with the sign of the Seven Stars in the middle of the seventeenth century suggest that a variety of businesses were involved in retailing wine. Just as Dekker exposed all manner of merchants for selling beer, in Tudor times the sale of wine was as indiscriminate. Part of the discrepancy between sign and function can be explained by a quote from André Simon's *History of the Wine Trade in England*:

> During the reign of Henry VII, and throughout the sixteenth century, any person was free to retail wine that had obtained a licence from the municipal authority. Freemen of the Vintners' Company, however, were not under the necessity of obtaining such a licence, since the first condition of their eligibility for the Company was that they should have been apprenticed to a Vintner and thus learned their trade.
>
> Such licences were also granted directly by the monarch, and, unfortunately, without enforcing the stipulated apprenticeship.
>
> Thus, in 1583, Queen Elizabeth granted licences for the retail of wine in London to two drapers, one mercer, two grocers, nine merchant-tailors, four haberdashers, four cloth-workers, three fishmongers, one chandler, two girdlers, and the widow of a barber-surgeon.
>
> Elizabeth granted a great many such licences, patents and monopolies, and although she renewed the Vintners' Charter in 1567, and again in 1577, she prefaced the latter with a statement which must have been very distasteful to the Company, to the effect that everyone was free "to pursue such lawful calling whereby he may gain his living, as is most agreeable to his choice or taste". At the same time she repeated and amplified a decree of Henry VIII to the effect that every freeman of the City of London, and the widows of such, were free to sell wine "in London, Southwark, and the liberties of our Duchy of Lancaster without Temple Bars in London".[2]

During Henry VIII's reign a number of members of the Vintner's Company were delegated every December to inspect the premises of anyone selling wine to ensure that it was of a required standard:

After proceeding with their search in the City, the searchers had to render an account of all the wines, good or bad, which they had found. These reports are, of course, very valuable on account of the indications they furnish regarding the stocks of wine and proportions of the different sorts of wine used in England at the time. They also bring additional proofs to the fact that many, besides Vintners, were licensed to sell wine in London. Among the keepers of taverns and cellars where defective wine was seized, the names of drapers, haberdashers, merchant taylors, tallow chandlers, coopers etc., are to be found, as well as, in fact, in a far greater proportion, than those of vintners and taverners.

There were also usually a few names of persons selling wine in cellars or taverns without a licence and being members of other companies than the Vintners. Thus, the list of persons retailing wine without a licence in December, 1568, included the following: "Roger Richardson, merchant taylor, for a cellar in the Strand, and another in Bermondsey Street; William Hamsworth, clothworker, for a house in Holborn, and another in Bermondsey Street; Thomas Parkyns, cooper, for a cellar at Aldgate and another in Seething Lane; David Maston, fishmonger, at the Dolphin, in New Fish Street; William Toughe, clothworker, at Bosom'd Inn; John Barber and Dominic Busher, 'estraungers,' etc." [3]

Most shops in the City of London would have consisted of more than one storey and it was possible to carry on the normal business at street level and have a tavern upstairs which required advertising. Having a free cellar might be even more convenient. If this was the situation in London, things would have been even more liberal in the far-flung provinces where official sanction was much more remote.

A number of people have assiduously catalogued the names of old taverns from such sources as the works of Shakespeare and Samuel Pepys' diaries. André Simon listed 114 London taverns from the fifteenth and sixteenth centuries based mainly on Guildhall records. None of these was called the Seven Stars. [4] These were all large, official taverns within the ambit of the Vintners' Company. They did not need to advertise what it was they sold. However, we know from the tokens issued during the middle of the seventeenth century that the sign of the Seven Stars was common in London, suggesting that drink, particularly wine, was much more widely available and this practice may have been going on for centuries. As André Simon says:

There was no town in England, either small or great, where wine could not be procured during the fourteenth century, as appears from the numerous contemporary travelling accounts still in existence.[5]

Before the start of the scientific revolution in the eighteenth century people at all levels of society were exposed to Neoplatonic ideas about the nature of the world that had originated in the Middle East and Eastern Mediterranean up to 2000 years before. These included beliefs in the transformation of materials, the four elements that formed nature, astrology and the microcosm-macrocosm duality in which what occurred in the heavens on a grand scale was reflected in the patterns seen down here on earth. Nobody would have objected to the visualisation of the Pleiades as a bunch of grapes. Whether they chose to use this as a sign for wine on an everyday level is, to some extent, speculation. However, it is difficult to fit the facts together in any other way.

There is clearly a hidden history behind many old pubs which has so far failed to reach the record books. Having said that, there may still be items preserved in the mass of old charters and local government returns that have so far slipped under the radar because, as isolated pieces of information, they have not attracted anybody's attention. Such facts may add to our knowledge of the history and heritage of English inns and taverns. In this rapidly changing world, the preservation of some of these for their symbolic history as much as their architectural features should not be ignored.

Opposite page: The Seven Stars, Ashton Old Road Manchester and its grapes. Coincidence? Or the preservation of old esoteric knowledge into the present day

APPENDICES

Appendix A: Seven Stars with claims to have had origins between the fourteenth and seventeenth centuries.

	Town	County	Date
Seven Stars	Falmouth	Cornwall	17th C
Seven Stars	Exeter	Devon	<16th C
Seven Stars Inn	South Tawton	Devon	17th C
Seven Stars	Tamerton Foliot	Devon	13th C
Royal Seven Stars	Totnes	Devon	<1486
Seven Stars	Brighton	Sussex	1535
Seven Stars	Robertsbridge	Sussex	14th C
Seven Stars	Canterbury	Kent	17th C
Seven Stars	Foots Cray	Kent	15th C
Seven Stars	Dawes Green	Surrey	16th C
Seven Stars	Farnham	Surrey	17th C
Seven Stars Inn	Bottlesford	Wiltshire	16th C
Seven Stars	Bristol	Gloucestershire	<17th C
Seven Stars	Dinton	Buckinghamshire	<1640
Seven Stars	Knowl Hill	Berkshire	17th C
Seven Stars	Carey Street	London	1602
Seven Stars	Marsh Baldon	Oxfordshire	<17th C
Seven Stars	Ledbury	Herefordshire	1526
Seven Stars Hotel	Warwick	Warwickshire	1585
Seven Stars	Ketley	Shropshire	1579
Seven Stars	Derby	Derbyshire	1680
Seven Stars	Brocton	Staffordshire	17th C
Ye Olde Seven Stars	Manchester	Lancashire	1356
Old Original Seven Stars	Leyland	Lancashire	1686

(Those in italics have closed in the last one hundred years — also shown as open dots in the image on page 38)

Appendix B: The distribution by counties of legal codes included in
the *Laws of William the Conqueror* (after Stenton, 1971).

West Saxon	Mercian	Danelaw
Kent	Oxfordshire	Buckinghamshire
Surrey	Warwickshire	Middlesex
Sussex	Gloucestershire	Essex
Berkshire	Worcestershire	Hertfordshire
Hampshire	Herefordshire	Bedfordshire
Wiltshire	Shropshire	Northamptonshire
Dorset	Staffordshire	Leicestershire
Somerset	Cheshire*	Cambridgeshire
Devon		Huntingdonshire
		Suffolk
		Norfolk
		Nottinghamshire
	* Including southern	Derbyshire
	Lancashire.	Lincolnshire
		Yorkshire

Appendix C: Seven Stars which were open in the year 2000 grouped by the Anglo-Saxon Law Codes.

	Town	County
Seven Stars	Falmouth	Cornwall
Seven Stars	Flushing	Cornwall
Seven Stars	Helston	Cornwall
Seven Stars	Penryn	Cornwall
Seven Stars Inn	Stithians	Cornwall
Seven Stars Inn	St Austell	Cornwall
Seven Stars	Exeter	Devon
Seven Stars	Tamerton Foliot	Devon
Royal Seven Stars	Totnes	Devon
Seven Stars Inn	South Tawton	Devon
Seven Stars	Winkleigh	Devon
Seven Stars	Kingsbridge	Devon
Seven Stars	Kennford	Devon
Seven Stars	Dartmouth	Devon
Seven Stars Inn	Wool	Dorset
Seven Stars	Timsbury	Somerset

Seven Stars Inn	Bottlesford	Wiltshire
Seven Stars	Winsley	Wiltshire
Seven Stars	Stroud	Hampshire
Seven Stars	Brighton	Sussex
Seven Stars	Robertsbridge	Sussex
Seven Stars	Canterbury	Kent
Seven Stars	Foots Cray	Kent
Seven Stars	Dawes Green	Surrey
Seven Stars	Farnham	Surrey
Seven Stars	Ripley	Surrey
Seven Stars	Holborn	London
Seven Stars	Brick Lane	London
Seven Stars	West Kensington	London
Seven Stars	Whitechapel	London
Seven Stars	Ascot	Berkshire
Seven Stars	Knowl Hill	Berkshire
Seven Stars	Marsh Baldon	Oxfordshire
Seven Stars	Bristol	Gloucestershire
Seven Stars	Ledbury	Herefordshire
Seven Stars	Clehonger	Herefordshire
Seven Stars	Cradley	Herefordahire
Seven Stars Inn	Aberdew	Powys
Seven Stars	Hay-on-Wye	Powys
Seven Stars	Wrexham	Denbighshire
Ye Olde Seven Stars	Kidderminster	Worcestershire
Seven Stars	Oldswinford	Worcestershire
Seven Stars	Redditch	Worcestershire
Seven Stars Hotel	Warwick	Warwickshire
Seven Stars	Sedgley	Warwickshire
Seven Stars	Rugby	Warwickshire
Seven Stars	Smethwick	Warwickshire
Seven Stars	Brocton	Staffordshire
Seven Stars Inn	Seisdon	Staffordshire
Seven Stars	Sandon Bank	Staffordshire
Seven Stars Inn	Old Coleham	Shropshire
Seven Stars	Shipton	Shropshire
Seven Stars	Beckbury	Shropshire
Seven Stars	Cold Hatton	Shropshire
Seven Stars Inn	Halfway House	Shropshire
Seven Stars	Thornton Hough	Cheshire
Seven Stars	Aston Old Road	Manchester
Seven Stars	Dantzic Street	Manchester

Old Original Seven Stars	Leyland	Lancashire
Seven Stars	Leyland	Lancashire
Seven Stars	Ashton-under-Lyne	Lancashire
Seven Stars Hotel	Barnoldswick	Lancashire
Seven Stars	Bury	Lancashire
Seven Stars	Chorley	Lancashire
Seven Stars Inn	Ecclesdon	Lancashire
Seven Stars	Harwood	Lancashire
Seven Stars	Little Lever	Lancashire
Seven Stars Hotel	Stalmine	Lancashire
Seven Stars	Dinton	Buckinghamshire
Seven Stars	Piddington	Buckinghamshire
Seven Stars	Cambridge	Cambridgeshire
Seven Stars	March	Cambridgeshire
Seven Stars	Derby	Derbyshire
Seven Stars	Belper	Derbyshire
Seven Stars	Riddings	Derbyshire
Seven Stars	Hucknall	Nottinghamshire
Seven Stars	Bradford	Yorkshire
Seven Stars	Guisborough	Yorkshire
Seven Stars Inn	Shincliffe	Durham
Seven Stars	Wreckenton	Durham
Seven Stars Hotel	Ponteland	Northumberland

Appendix D: Kings of England (or at least part of it) from Alfred the Great to the Conquest.

Alfred the Great	871- 899	Swein Forkbeard	1013-1014
Edward the Elder	899- 924	Æthelred	1014-1016
Athelstan	924- 939	Edmund Ironside	1016
Edmund I	939- 946	Cnut	1016-1035
Eadred	946- 955	Harold I	1035-1040
Eadwig	955- 959	Harthacnut	1040-1042
Edgar	959- 975	Edward the Confessor	1042-1066
Edward	975- 978	Harold II	1066
Æthelred	978-1013	William of Normandy	1066-1087

NOTES

Chapter 1. The Origins of the Pub
1. Dietrich, et al. (2012): pp. 667ff.
2. Nissen et al. 1993: pp. 36-46.
3. Collon (2005): pp. 27 and 148, nos. 91 and 640.
4. Laurence (1994): pp. 70-87.
5. Cunliffe (2013): pp. 327 and 361-2.
6. Dornbusch (1997): pp. 90-6.
7. Nilson (1998): pp. 210-11.
8. Bruning and Paulin (1982): p. 20.
9. Clark (1983): pp. 195, 215 and 298.

Chapter 2. Inn Signs
1. Cox (1994): p. 8.
2. Haydon (1994): p. 186.
3. Meiggs (1973): pp. 429-30 and Pl. XXIXb.
4. Firebaugh (1923): pp. 157-8. Beard (2008): p. 60.
5. Mau (1902): p. 400.
6. Beard (2008): pp. 20 and 225.
7. Firebaugh (1923): p. 159.
8. Endell (1916): p. 29.
9. Cox (1994): p. 11.
10. Monckton (1969): pp. 29-30.
11. Haydon (1994): p. 23.
12. Trum (2002): p. 6.
13. Monckton (1969): p. 57.
14. Liungman (1991): p. 464.
15. Trum (2002): p. 7.
16. Trum (2002): p. 8.
17. Liungman (1991): pp. 300-2.

Chapter 3. Seven Stars
1. Seven Stars inn signs from top left by row: Riddings; Carey Street, London; Knowl Hill; Totnes; Bottlesford; South Tawton; Canterbury; Aston Old Road, Manchester; Ledbury; Helston; Dinton; Tamerton Foliot; Marsh Baldon; Redditch; Derby; Stithians.
2. Rogers (1935): p. 114.
3. McGrath and Williams (1979): pp. 39-40.
4. Cottingham (2000).
5. Harper (1906): vol. I, pp. 6-12.
6. William Harrison Ainsworth (1805-82), a Victorian novelist who wrote a successful book called *Guy Fawkes* in 1841.
7. Harvey (2011): p. 79.
8. Harvey (2011): p. 65.
9. Presswell (1963): pp 4-8.
10. McGrath and Williams (1979): pp. vi-vii.
11. Dening (1949): p. 112.
12. Clarkson (1808): pp. 322-4, 350.
13. Pinches (2009): pp. 28ff. This is part of the updated Victoria County History series and is the most up to date history of Ledbury from Tudor times onwards. Much about recent events

at the Seven Stars can be found in the archives of the *Hereford Times.*
14. Sturley (1990).
15. Mock (2012): pp. 27-33.
16. Lega-Weeks (1907): p. 313; and (1909): p. 365.
17. Wilmot (1988): p. 70. Kent Archives Office CCA-CC-WOODRUFFS/16/22.
18. Kent Archives Office CCA-CC-J/A/31743/2. Also see Kolb (2013): p. 230.
19. *Leyland. Historic Town Assessment Report.* (Lancashire County Council, Preston, 2006).
20. Moore (2018).
21. Robb (2013): pp. 40-64 and 281.
22. Turner and Dobrzynski (2007): pp. 113-4.
23. Trumper (2001): p. 35.
24. Plymouth Public Library Photo Collection. Plymouth Images Folder 45. Public Houses. P728.5 SEV. Record No. 000102032. Photo by M. J. Crew 1966. 11.5 x 16.5 cm.
25. Tanner (1979): p. 2.
26. Palmer (1991): p. 16.
27. Hogg (1974): p. 27.

Chapter 4. The Immaculate Conception
1. Warner (1976): pp. 93f and Fig. 11.
2. Hinnells (1988): pp. 68-70. See also Nigosian (1993): pp. 94-7.

Chapter 5. The Book of Enoch
1. A full account of the Mesopotamian myths can be found in Dalley (1989). Their relation to the calendar can be found in J.M. Steele, *The Length of the Month in Mesopotamian Calendars of the First Millenium* BC, in Steele, ed. (2007): pp. 133-148.
2 Dalley (1989): p. 275 n. 28. The more common word was *shapattu*, usually written in Sumerian logograms as **ud 15 kam** which literally means day number fifteen. According to Genesis, Abraham stayed in Harran before moving on to Canaan. Harran was famous throughout the ancient Middle East as a centre for moon worship (see Tamara Green, *The City of the Moon God,* (Leyden, 1992)). The early Jews seem to have adapted the Mesopotamian cultic cycle to their own uses by changing from a thirty to a twenty-eight day month, just as the months of the Jewish calendar are almost identical with those used in ancient Mesopotamia.
3. This translation is from Charles (1893): pp. 43 and 47. A more modern version can be found in Charlesworth (1983). The patchwork nature of *I Enoch* means that several passages are often repeated with a slightly different content. In the quotations some of these have been edited together.

Chapter 6. The Masons
1. Stone (2015): p. 55.
2. Stevenson (1988): pp. 19-21.

3. Curl (1991): Ch. 1-3.
4. Knoop and Jones (1947): pp. 153-203.
5. Knoop, Jones and Hamer (1945): p. 287. An example of the Seven Stars' leet court references can be found in the Kent County Archives CCA-CC-J/A/3/1743/2.

Chapter 7. The Solar System
1. Black et al. (2004): pp. 63-76.

Chapter 8. The Plough
1. Allen (1963): p. 431.
2. Kolb (2013): pp. 153-6 and Fig. 37.
3. Allen (1963): p. 43.
4. Riley and Eley, 1983: p. 3.

Chapter 9. The Seven Stars of Taurus
1. Andrews (2004).
2. Hunger and Pingree (1989): p. 30; verse i.44. MUL.APIN translates as the Plough Star but this was a Babylonian name for an entirely different star or constellation to the modern one.
3. Black and Green (1998): fig. 134, p. 163.
4. Black and Green (1998): p. 162. It has to be said that a rosette is a basic pattern that can be easily achieved with a drill and some Mittanean seals have rosettes with more than seven dots in them.
5. van der Wearden (1974): p. 80.
6. Allen (1963): p. 397.

Chapter 10. Stars and Monasteries
1. Principe (2013): pp. 69-71. The ancient Greeks also had a fifth element which was different. Plato was clear that there were four elements and he associated them with regular geometric bodies: Fire with the tetrahedron, Earth with the cube, Air with the octahedron and Water with the icosahedron. Later Neoplatonists were aware that there was another regular solid, the dodecahedron, and they associated this with another element 'Aether'. This was a much more nebulous geometric and philosophical concept and nobody really understood what it was. It never had any role in practical alchemy.
2. Kerenyi (1976): p. 67.
3. Goodenough (1953): Vols. 1 & 3.
4. Jewish Encyclopaedia Vol. VIII (New York, 1904). Goodenough (1958): Vol. 7 for a discussion of rosettes and Greek magical signs.
5. Goodenough (1956): Vol. 4, pp. 65f.
6. Encyclopaedia Judaica (Jerusalem, 1972): Vol. 16, p.543.

Chapter 11. The Anglo-Saxons and the Danes
1. The sequence of kings up until the Norman Conquest is slightly obscure for many and is outlined in Appendix D.

2. Stenton (1971): pp. 505ff.
3. The story, probably apocryphal, is that Gregory saw some fair-haired Anglo-Saxon slaves for sale in Rome and asked who they were. When he was told that they were Angles he said: 'Not Angles, but Angels' and promptly sent Augustine and forty monks to convert the English.
4. Stenton (1971): pp. 502–25.
5. Hart (1992): pp. 20-23. A half mark equalled 80 pence, and 1 ore equalled 16 pence.
6. Harding (1978): pp. 144-168.

Chapter 12. The Celestial Grapes
1. Kolb (2013): pp. 233-4 and Fig. 46.
2. Bowra (1961): pp. 316-7.
3. Thompson (1936): pp. 210 and 225-31.
4. Allen (1963): p. 396.
5. Kolb (2013): Ch. 5 and 6. See also www.foxesfromthegods.com.
6. Leonidas *Greek Anthology*: 9.99; Martial *Epigrams*: III.24.
7. Boardman (2001): pp. 32 and 99, and Pl. 43.
8. Varro *On Agriculture* I.II.18 and II.III.7.
9. Perry (1965): pp. xlvii-l and 139 -141.
10. Kolb (2013): pp. 164-5.
11. Kolb (2013): pp. 40-43 and 69-86.
12. Bivar (1969): p. 26 and Pl. 11 Fig DZ 1.
13. Hagen (1995): pp. 204-07.
14. Stenton (1971): p. 288. Bickerdyke (1889): p. 185.
15. Hagen (1995): pp. 335-6.
16. Campbell (2000): pp. 96-100, 120 and 162.
17. Cunliffe (2013): pp. 441-3 and Fig. 12.25.
18. Cunliffe (2001): pp. 386-91 and 417-21.
19. Hagen (1995): pp. 223-4.
20. Simon (1906): pp. 14-7.

Conclusions
1. Simon (1907): pp. 102-10.
2. Simon (1907): pp. 78-9.
3. Simon (1907): pp. 97-8.
4. Simon (1907): Appendix C, pp. 321-6.
5. Simon (1906): p. 359.

BIBLIOGRAPHY

Allen, R.H. *Star Names. Their Lore and Meaning* (New York, 1963).

Andrews. M. *The Seven Sisters of the Pleiades. Stories from around the world* (Melbourne, 2004).

Beard, M. *Pompeii. The Life of a Roman Town* (London, 2008).

Bickerdyke, J. *The Curiosities of Ale and Beer. An Entertaining History* (London, 1889).

Biva, A.D.H. *Catalogue of Western Asian Seals in the British Museum. Stamp Seals II. The Sassanian Dynasty* (London, 1969).

Black, J., Cunningham, G., Robson, E., and Zolyomi, G. *The Literature of Ancient Sumer* (Oxford, 2004).

Black, J. and Green, A. *Gods, Demons and Symbols of Ancient Mesopotamia* (London, 1998).

Boardman, J. *Greek Gems and Finger Rings. Early Bronze Age to Late Classical* (London, 2001).

Bowra, C.M. *Greek Lyric Poetry. From Alcman to Simonides* (Oxford, 1961).

Bruning, T. and Paulin, K. *Historic English Inns* (Newton Abbot, 1982).

Campbell, J. *The Anglo-Saxon State* (London, 2000).

Charles, R.H. *The Book of Enoch* (Oxford, 1893).

Charlesworth, J.H. *The Old Testament Pseudepigraphica Vol. 1* (London, 1983).

Clark, P. *The English Alehouse: a social history 1200-1830* (London, 1983).

Clarkson, T. *The History of the Rise, Progress and Accomplishment of the Abolition of the African Slave-Trade by the British Parliament. Vol. I* (London, 1808).

Collon, D. *First Impressions. Cylinder Seals in the Ancient Near East* (London, 2005).

Cottingham, A. *The Hostelries of Henley* (Shiplake, 2000).

Cox, B. *English Inn and Tavern Names* (Nottingham, 1994).

Cunliffe, B. *Facing the Ocean. The Atlantic and Its Peoples* (Oxford, 2001).

Cunliffe, B. *Britain Begins* (Oxford, 2013).

Curl, J.S. *The Art and Architecture of Freemasonry* (London, 1991).

Dalley, S. *Myths from Mesopotamia. Creation, The Flood, Gilgamesh and Others* (Oxford, 1989).

Dening, C.F.W. *Old Inns of Bristol* (Bristol, 1949).

Dietrich, O., Heun, M., Notroff, J., Schmidt, K. and Zarnkow, M. "The role of cult and feasting in the emergence of Neolithic communities. New evidence from Göbekli Tepe, south-eastern Turkey." *Antiquity* 86 (2012): 674-695.

Dornbusch, H.D. *Prost! The Story of German Beer* (Boulder, 1997).

Endell, F. *Old Tavern Signs. An Excursion in the History of Hospitality* (Cambridge, 1916).

Firebaugh, W.C. *The Inns of Greece and Rome* (Chicago, 1923).

Goodenough, E.R. *Jewish Symbols of the Greco-Roman Period* (New York, 1953-1958).

Hagen, A. *A Handbook of Anglo-Saxon Food and Drink. Production and Distribution* (Hockwold cum Wilton, 1995).

Harding, A. *Early trailbaston proceedings from the Lincoln Rolls of 1305*, in Meekings, C.A.F. *Medieval Legal Records* (London, 1978).

Harper, C.G. *The Old Inns of England* (London, 1906).

Hart, C. *The Danelaw* (London, 1992).

Harvey, H. *The Story of Exeter* (Andover, 2011).

Haydon, P. *The English Pub. A History* (London, 1994).

Hinnells, J.R. *Persian Mythology* (London, 1988).

Hogg, G. *The English Country Inn* (London, 1974).

Hunger, H. and Pingree, D. *MUL.APIN. An Astronomical Compendium in Cuneiform* (Horn, 1989).

Hunter, J. *English Inns, Taverns, Alehouses and Brandy Shops: The Legislative Framework, 1495-1797.* In: *The World of the Tavern.* Ed. Beat Kümin and B. Ann Tlusty (Aldershot, 2002).

Knoop, D and Jones, G.P. *The Genesis of Freemasonry* (Manchester, 1947).

Knoop, D., Jones, G.P. and Hamer, D. *Early Masonic Pamphlets* (Manchester, 1945).

Kerenyi, C. *Dionysos. Archetypal Image of Indestructible Life* (Princeton, 1976).

Kolb, H.H. *Foxes from the Gods* (Logie Coldstone, 2013).

Larwood, J. and Hotten, J.C. *The History of Signboards from the Earliest Times to the Present Day* (London, 1866).

Larwood, J. and Hotten, J.C. *English Inn Signs* (Exeter, 1985).

Laurence, R. *Roman Pompeii, Space and Society* (London, 1994).

Lega-Weeks, E. "The Church Wardens Accounts of South Tawton, Pt. II." *Transactions of the Devonshire Association* (1907): pp. 302-336.

Lega-Weeks, E. "Introduction to the Church Wardens Accounts of South Tawton." *Transactions of the Devonshire Association* (1909): pp. 361-7.

Lillywhite, B. *London Signs. A Reference Book of London Signs from Earliest Times to about the Mid-nineteenth Century* (London, 1972).

Liungman, C.G. *Dictionary of Symbols* (New York, 1991).

Mau, A. *Pompeii. Its Life and Art* (London, 1902).

McGrath, P. and Williams, M.E. *Bristol Inns and Alehouses in the Mid-Eighteenth Century* (Bristol, 1979).

Meiggs, R. *Roman Ostia* (Oxford, 1973).

Mock, J. *Bradford on Avon's Pubs and Breweries* (Bradford on Avon, 2012).

Monckton, H.A. *A History of the English Public House* (London, 1969).

Moore, N. *A History of Blackpool, the Fylde and South Wyre* (Blackpool, 2018).

Nigosian, S.A. *The Zoroastrian Faith. Tradition & Modern Research* (Montreal, 1993).

Nilson, B. *Cathedral Shrines of Medieval England* (Woodbridge, 1998).

Nissen, H.J., Damerow, P. and Englund, R.K. *Archaic Bookkeeping. Early Writing and Techniques of Economic Administration in the Ancient Near East* (Chicago, 1993).

Palmer, J. *Penryn in the Eighteenth Century* (Truro, 1991).

Paoli, U.E. *Rome. Its People, Life and Customs* (London, 1963).

Perry, B.E. *Babrius and Phaedrus* (London, 1965).

Pinches, S. *Ledbury, a market town and its Tudor heritage* (Chichester, 2009).

Presswell, P. *A History of the Royal Seven Stars Hotel, Totnes, Devon* (Totnes, 1963).

Principe, L.M. *The Secrets of Alchemy* (Chicago, 2013).

Riley, R.C. and Eley, P. *Public Houses and Beerhouses in Nineteenth Century Portsmouth. The Portsmouth Papers No. 38* (Portsmouth, 1983).

Robb, G. *The Ancient Paths. Discovering the Lost Map of Celtic Europe* (London, 2013).

Rogers, K. *Old London: Cornhill, Threadneedle Street and Lombard Street, Old Houses and Signs* (London, 1935).

Simon, A.L. *The History of the Wine Trade in England Vol. 1.* (London, 1906).

Simon, A.L. *The History of the Wine Trade in England Vol. 2.* (London, 1907).

Steele, J.M. (ed.) *Calendars and Years. Astronomy and Time in the Ancient Near East* (Oxford, 2007).

Stenton, F.M. *Anglo-Saxon England.* (Oxford, 1971).

Stevenson, D. *The Origins of Freemasonry. Scotland's Century 1590-1710* (Cambridge, 1988).

Stone, B. *Bonnie Prince Charlie and the Highland Army in Derby* (Comford, 2015).

Sturley M. *The Breweries and Public Houses of Guildford II* (Guildford, 1990).

Tanner, K. *Old Kingsbridge Inns. Cookworthy Papers 5* (Kingsbridge, 1979).

Thompson, D.W. *A Glossary of Greek Birds* (Oxford, 1936).

Trum, M. *Historische Darstellung, Zundtzeichen und Symbole des Braue- und Mälzerhandwerks* (Munich, 2002).

Trumper, D. *Telford. Britain in Old Photographs* (Stroud, 2001).

Turner, K. and Dobrzynski, J. *Worcestershire's Historic Pubs* (Stroud, 2007).

van der Waerden, B.L. *Science Awakening II. The Birth of Astronomy* (Leyden, 1974).

Warner, M. *Alone of All Her Sex. The Myth and Cult of the Virgin Mary* (London, 1976).

Webb, D. *Pilgrimage in Medieval England* (London, 2000).

Webb, S. and B. *The History of Liquor Licensing* (London, 1903).

Wilmot, E. *Inns of Canterbury* (Canterbury, 1988).

INDEX

Seven Stars

Belper	109, 232
Bottlesford	79-80, 229, 231, 233
Bradford-on-Avon	80-1, 232, 236
Brighton	35, 74-6, 229, 231
Bristol	58-61, 169, 172, 229, 231, 235-6
Canterbury	89-93, 173, 229, 231, 233, 237
Clehonger	66-7, 231
Clifton	47
Dartmouth	57, 222, 230
Dawes Green	67-9, 203, 229, 231
Derby	106-7, 169, 210, 229, 232-3
Dinton	35, 86-7, 210, 229, 232-3
Exeter	49-53, 169, 229, 230
Falmouth	37, 116-7, 210, 229, 230
Farnham	69-70, 229, 231
Flushing	120-1, 230
Foots Cray	8, 76-7, 127, 229, 231
Guildford	69
Hay-on-Wye	66-7, 231
Helston	119-20, 230, 233
Henley	37, 235
Ketley	112, 229
Kidderminster	109-10, 231
Knowl Hill	78-9, 169, 229, 231, 233
Larkhill	46
Ledbury	62-5, 229, 231, 233
Leyland	103-4, 229, 232
London	35, 95-102, 210, 229, 231, 233
Manchester	4, 39-48, 79, 155, 169, 227-33
Marsh Baldon	82-3, 229, 231, 233
Penryn	118-9, 126, 230
Plymouth	36, 113-5
Redditch	111, 231, 233
Riddings	108, 200, 232-3
Ripley	69-70, 231
Robertsbridge	6, 71-3, 229, 231
Salford	46
South Tawton	84-5, 200, 229-30, 233
Stalmine	105, 232
St Austell	122-5, 230
Stifford's Bridge	65
Stithians	120-1, 230, 233
St Just in Roseland	120
Stroud	87-8, 231
Tamerton Folio	36, 113-5, 200, 229-30, 233
Totnes	53-6, 229-30, 233, 237
Warwick	111, 229, 231
Winsley	80-1, 231

Plough Inns

Derby	107, 169
Museum Street, London	166, 169
Kensal Green, London	169
Norwood Green, Middlesex	169
Rosemarkie, Cromarty	169, 171
Sittingbourne, Kent	169

Public Houses and Inns

Apple Tree Tavern, London	153
At Checker of the Hope, Canterbury	28, 89, 91-2
Bingley Arms, Bardsey	17
Black Lion, Weston	19
Blue Anchor, Helston	120
Bull Inn, London	98
Bull's Head, Salford	41
Carpenter's Arms, York	153
Cherub, Dartmouth	57-8
Cheshire Cheese, London	153
Court House Tavern, Kidderminster	109
Crown, Canterbury	92
Crown Alehouse, London	153
Crown and Anchor, London	153
Devil, London	153
Elephant and Castle, Ketley	112
Falstaff, Canterbury	91
Feathers, Ledbury	63-4
Fox and Seven Stars, Canterbury	92
Fox and Seven Stars, London	173-4
George Hotel, Robertsbridge	71
Godbegot, Winchester	17
Goose and Gridiron, London	153
Half Moon and Seven Stars, Preston	163, 181
Horn Tavern, London	153
Horse and Groom, Guildford	69
King's Arms, London	153
King's Head, Kidderminster	109
Leg and Seven Stars, London	97
London Inn, St Austell	123
Masonic Tavern, London	154
Morning Star, Portsmouth	164, 172
Nag's Head and Star, Carmarthen	153
Old Plough Inn, Kensal Green	169
Ostrich, Colnbrook	16-7
Oxenham Arms, South Zeal	84
Prancing Pony, Stiffords Bridge	65
Queen's Head, London	153
Red Lion, Canterbury	91-2, 153
Rose, Canterbury	92
Rummer and Grapes, London	153
Saracen's Head, Canterbury	92
Ship, Leyland	103
Star, Rusper	187
Sun, Canterbury	92
Swan, Chichester	153
Talbot, Ledbury	63-4
Three Compasses, London	153
Three Kings, Canterbury	92

Three Tuns, Kidderminster — 109
Wellington Inn, Manchester — 41, 46
White Hart, Canterbury — 92
Ye Olde Dolphin, Derby — 107
Ye Olde Trip to Jerusalem, Nottingham — 17-8, 57, 128
Ye Olde Rovers Return, Manchester — 41

Pub Names

Angel — 128
Bell on the Hoop — 28
Bishop's Head — 128
Cardinal's Hat — 128
Chequers — 91
Compasses — 155
Fox and Goose — 173
Freemason's Arms — 154-5
George — 22
George on the Hoop — 28
Half Moon — 163, 172
Hand-in-Hand — 93
Hearts of Oak — 172
Lamb and Flag — 128
Le Cock in the Hoop — 28
Le Sonne on the Hoop — 163
Lord Nelson — 172
Mayflower — 172
Mermaid — 172
New Inn — 22
Polar Star — 172
Pope's Head — 128
Plough and Flail — 169
Plough and Furrow — 169
Plough and Harrow — 169
Plough and Horses — 169
Salutation — 128
Sun — 22
Tabard — 22

People

Adam — 145
Addison, Joseph — 173
Aesop — 22, 211, 216
Æthelbert of Kent — 217
Æthelred II — 80, 206, 209, 218, 232
Æthelstan, King — 218
Alfred the Great — 54, 79, 205-10, 232
Anaxagoras — 163
Aratus — 158, 171
Aristotle — 168, 187
Atlas — 175-6, 183, 185, 213
Aubrey, John — 198
Babrius — 216
Bacchus — 26-7, 41, 174, 195, 214
Becket, Thomas à — 89, 113

Beckford, Walter — 116
Bede, Venerable — 212, 221
Benedict of Nursia — 17, 197
Bonnie Prince Charlie — 46, 152
Bruegel, Peter — 32
Brown, Tom — 92
Browning, Elizabeth Barrett — 65
Butler, Samuel — 163
Cassius Dio — 164
Catullus — 24
Charles I — 86
Charles II — 72
Charlemagne — 220
Chaucer, Geoffrey — 29-31, 89, 191-3
Clarkson, Thomas — 59-61
Cnut (Canute), King — 17, 206-9, 212, 218, 232
Constantine — 131, 205
Copernicus — 162, 165
Cranmer, Thomas — 91
Cyril of Alexandria — 128
Defoe, Daniel — 14, 55-7
Dekker, Thomas — 15, 30-1, 204, 223-4
Dionysos — 26, 195, 213, 216
Dolci, Carlo — 139
Dumuzid — 159-61
Dürer, Albrecht — 135-6, 142, 145
Edgar, King — 16, 54, 206, 217, 232
Edmund Ironside — 206, 232
Edmund, King — 17, 54, 207-8, 232
Eadred of Wessex — 219
Edward I — 200, 210
Edward III — 41, 45
Edward VI — 91
Edward the Confessor — 218, 232
Elizabeth I — 67, 91, 96, 224
Empedocles — 189
Enki — 144, 159
Enoch — 141, 145-9
Euclid — 152
Eudoxus of Cnidos — 157
Eve — 137, 152
Evelyn, John — 36-7
Fale, Thomas — 167
Fawkes, Guy — 42-3
Forster, I.T.M. — 173
Fox, George — 49
Galileo — 163
Geoffrey of Monmouth — 53
George IV — 74
Giotto — 129-30, 136
Goethe — 32-3
Hadrian — 164
Hammurabi, King — 11
Harper, Charles — 7, 39-44

Harthacnut, King	220, 232
Harold, King	84, 232
Helios	130
Henry I	84
Henry III	29, 95
Henry VII	55, 224
Henry VIII	13, 18, 91, 116, 200, 224
Hermes	25, 152, 185, 192, 213
Herod	129
Hesiod	175, 183-4
Hogarth, William	14
Homer	53, 175
Hotten, John Camden	7, 19, 22, 151
Hyginus	176
Inana	159-61
Ine of Wessex	218
Isaiah	127
Isidore of Seville	215
Jack the Ripper	101
Jan van Eyck	132-3
Jerome K. Jerome	20
John of Rupescissa	188
John, King	120
Jonson, Ben	67-9
Joseph	127-9
Josephus, Flavius	152
Jupiter	158-9, 193
Kepler	162
Larwood, Jacob	7, 22, 35, 151, 164
Leonidas of Tarentum	215
Lillywhite, Bryant	7, 35-6, 155, 169, 181
Marduk	144
Masefield, John	65
Milton, John	162-3
Mosely, Oswald	99
Noah	145, 147, 152
Orion	158, 183-5, 213
Ovid	215
Parmenides	162
Pasteur, Louis	197
Peirce, Charles Sanders	21
Pepys, Samuel	7, 225
Phaedrus	22
Philo of Alexandria	143
Plato	149, 152, 155, 192-3, 200, 226
Plautus	24
Pliny, the Elder	12
Ptolemy of Alexandria	157, 161-2
Pythagoras	152, 162, 190
Raleigh, Walter	116
Richard II	30
Rummynge, Eleanor	198-9
Severus, Septimius	164
Shakespeare, William	7, 24, 26, 68-9, 225
Sharp, Cecil	14
Simon, André	13, 203, 221, 224-6
Simonides	213
Skelton, John	198-9
Smith, Sydney	15
Smollett, Tobias	19
Southey, Robert	117
St Alban	17-8, 136, 152
St Anne	128-9, 137
St Augustine of Canterbury	17
St Augustine of Hippo	89, 137
St Bonaventure	136, 139, 144
St Dunstan	89
St Edmund	17, 207-8, 210
St Germain	197
St John the Evangelist	133, 139, 141-2, 147
St Lawrence	33
St Martin	197
St Remi	197
Stephen, King	62
Swein Forkbeard	206, 232
Syrus, Publius	26
Tamuz	160-1
Taylor, John	13, 163, 170
Theon of Alexandria	215
Thompson, D'Arcy Wentworth	213-4
Tolkien, J.R.R.	65
Valentine, Brother Basil	190-2
Varro, Marcus Terentius	24, 216
Velázquez, Diego	138-9
Venus	137, 157-64, 176-9, 193, 215
Victoria, Queen	63
Villeneuve, Arnaud de	188
Virgin Mary	55, 76, 127-40, 145
Walpole, Horace	73
Wilberforce, William	59
William III	14, 56
William of Malmesbury	221
William the Conqueror	84, 204-7, 230, 232
Winstanley, William	28
Wulfstan, Archbishop	206, 209, 218
Wycliffe, John	89